To Ann,

Sept '93

For all your help
and understanding
Thank you.
Davy, March,
Andrew & Jill

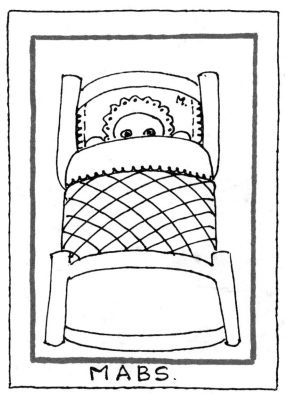

MABS.

GOOD MORROW BROTHER

DEDICATED
To my Grandsons
Hilary
Christian
and
Vivian Ziar

ROSEMERGY.

'GOOD MORROW BROTHER'

Written

and

Illustrated

by

ROSEMARY ZIAR

The day-to-day experience of West Cornwall life a century ago gave Mabel Trembath tales to tell her family. These became the inspiration for Rosemary Ziar's own folk stories. Storytelling pursues no literal truth, rather it reflects more generally on human nature while recalling experiences for the lessons they contained. Rosemary's stories joyfully recall a time now slipping off the edge of memory.
Toni Carver – November 1991

LEVANT

First Edition published December 1991.

© Rosemary Ziar.

Designed by Toni Carver.

Produced and Printed by
St. Ives Printing & Publishing Company,
High Street, St. Ives, Cornwall TR26 1RS.
Telephone: (0736) 795813.

ISBN 0 948385 14 6 (PAPERBACK)

ISBN 0 948385 16 2 (HARD COVER)

Acknowledgements and my thanks to: Toni Carver – who made this publication possible – my family, friends and Aunt Mabel Trembath who's memories and stories inspired this book.

CONTENTS

ZENNOR CHURCH.

ANNIE MAY & THE DEVIL? MAYBE?

ANNIE MAY sat on a bank beside the road between Morvah and Zennor, looking down the hill towards the village. The weather was beautiful. On such a day angels were born, so the old people said, and the little white clouds scudding across the sky were their swaddling clothes which they had thrown away.

The sun shone on the church amongst the May trees and on the dark green hedgerows of Escallonias. The pub cuddled close to the cob cottages scattered between the grey granite rocks. Great rocks they were, some of them as big as the cottages. One in particular stood out like an enormous round animal curled up asleep beside the road, hiding the old church door from Annie May's view. By midsummer, all being well, she would walk up the steps and through that door, on the arm of her father, for she was to be married to Willie Olds, a fine looking chap – a miner's son from over Levant way – with hair as black as a chough's underwing and eyes as blue as the moorland bluebells nodding behind her back. The May trees in their splendour were as white as her wedding dress folded away with a lavender bag in blue tissue paper in grandma's drawer. The dress had been her mother's who had died the very day Annie May was born. Her father never really forgave Annie May for having been born on that cold May day. He said no human being should do such a thing . . . no human being should come and take away his only love and expect love in return . . . goodness knows where the child came from or where she would end up . . . possibly with the Devil himself maybe!

Annie May looked down at the pub. It was almost closing time, and her father wouldn't be long. He was going to give her a ride home in his water-waggon at least part of the way; for the rest she would have to walk on to Pendeen from the Geevor turning.

The pub door was open now and a steady stream of men and dogs came up the hill, but there was no sign of father. As she shaded her eyes to see the better there was a swoosh and a woosh and a clatter of horses' hooves. Out from behind the great grey rock a covered wagon came charging up the hill, its red and gold wheels flashing and spinning with sparks flying, scattering the hens and gleenies under the farmer's gate. T'wernt father though, but a fine great man in a crimson cape with the reddest hair Annie May had ever seen, hair as red as a hawthorn berry, and eyes as black as sloes.

When he saw her he pulled the horses to a dead stop and jumped down.

"You must be Annie May, William Henry Oaté's maid," he said.

Annie May blushed, turned away and pulled her skirt well down over her knees. Had she been showing her white drawers, she wondered, or a peep of pink leg above her black stockings . . .?

With a mocking smile on his face the stranger said: "Come away to the ends of the Earth with me, my little May flower."

Annie May shook her bonnet.

"Well then, I'll give you a lift back to Granny's. Your father won't leave the pub till sundown, and you can't sit here all day. Come on, jump up with me, my love."

Annie May was in a fix. She was half afraid to say yes. She had been warned about strangers. In fact great-aunt Tregear said that the Devil himself rode around these parts seeing what he could be up to next; but Annie May wanted to be home in time for dinner. She was beginning to feel a bit leery under her pinny, and grand-ma made pasties on Thursdays.

"Come on." wheedled the stranger, "It won't take long."

So up she got and away they went – fast as the wind – to Pendeen Square. Well, they stopped by Rosemergy to pick a few sea-pinks for Granny, so it took a bit longer. Long enough some said afterwards.

Annie May and Willie Olds were married in Zennor Church on Midsummer's Day and lived to be old and crotchety like you and me and the rest of us. They had a fine family – three girls with black winged hair and eyes as blue as the moorland bluebells, but the firstborn was a boy with hair as red as a hawthorn berry and eyes as black as sloes . . .

ZENNOR FARM.

A GLEENY.

8

CHAPTER TWO

THE SEVENTH GRACE

IT WAS a muggy, clammy, silent night – the sort of weather that comes before Christmas in Pendeen. The miners, coming up from the last shift couldn't see their hands in front of their faces.

Maddern Trembath trudged up the hill. It had been a heavy day; not much sleep tonight by the looks of it he thought as he turned through the gate. He could see a dim light in Grace's bedroom window. The baby was expected soon. Would it be a son, he wondered, as he went up the path to the front door, or another girl?

Mabel, the first born, was only eleven months old. He could hear her crying in the kitchen. A happy sight met his eye as he entered. The kettles, black and shining, were singing on the slab whose brass knobs were glowing in the light of the oil lamp on the well-laid table which was groaning with food. Bread and butter, cold pork and pickles, marinated pilchards, heavy cake and Grandma's saffron buns.

Mrs. Curtis, from next door but one, was poking up the fire.

"How's she been?" he asked.

"Going on alright" she replied. "It will be a girl, Maddern. She's taking a long time to make up her mind to come. Grace has been up there oohing and aahing since you left this morning. You had better go up and see her before you have your tea. I'll give little Mabel her milk and sugar in her bottle before we sit down to have ours."

Maddern took his boots off and put them to dry on the rim of the fender. Mabel gave him a queer sort of look over the edge of her cradle. Knowing for one so young, he thought.

When Mabel was born last November, on the same sort of night as this, Grace had had a hard and long labour. Afterwards, as she lay looking up at him over the folded counterpane, she said in a very small voice:

"I'm going to call her Mabel."

All bedlam was let loose at the Christening. The baby was the last in line, the seventh Grace. The Trembaths could not believe their ears when old Reverend Rogers said:

"I baptize thee Mabel."

Great-aunt Trembath stalked out of Pendeen Church, Grandpa Trembath sidling along behind her. His dog Bessie scuttled between the parson's legs, knocking over the brass water ewer on the font steps and Mary Liz, the Godmother, nearly dropped Mabel into the font when she took her from the parson.

Grace's mother stood her ground. Ill luck there might be (not to continue the name of Grace for the seventh generation was considered

THE OLD BARN OWL.

hooting cry like the old barn owl up in the loft, and a tiny wail of a pee-wee.

"My soul, quick Mrs. Curtis, she's here."

Up the stairs they clattered and in through the bedroom door. Yes, it was a girl, big, red and shining, with a head of black curls and huge pansy brown eyes.

When things were straight, and Mrs. Curtis back again in the kitchen, Maddern looked down at Grace as she lay looking up at him over the folded counterpane. In a very loud and determined voice he said;

"For God's sake call her Grace."
And Grace my Mother was called.

PENDEEN FONT.

unheard of in the family circle and most unlucky) but if Grace wanted to call her first child Mabel, Mabel it would be and no Trembath could change it. "A lot of pop and touse," she said afterwards, "about nothing." The Trembath side of the family never spoke to the Oates side for nearly a year. They were a very superstitious and narrow-minded lot.

Maddern put on his slippers and made for the kitchen door, but it was too late. There was a long

CHAPTER THREE

AUNT TREGEAR'S 50th BIRTHDAY PARTY

PENDEEN summer evenings are long and warm. The sun sets late, like a great red ball of fire over the north western sea, the air is full of coconut scent from the yellow gorse bushes under the long ultramarine shadows of 'Five Old Hats,' the name given to Carn Kenidjack by Pendeen people.

On such an evening Aunt Tregear decided to give a supper party to celebrate her 50th birthday, asking all the family (not the Trembaths, mind you, as they hadn't been speaking again lately). However, she did ask Maddern and Grace. She had a soft spot for Maddern. He was a fine looking man with a good tenor voice, accompanying himself on his grandpa's concertina. He, with his

FIVE OLD HATS.

brother Matthew blowing on an old "push'n to and pull'n from 'ee," gave great pleasure at many a party. Maddern and Grace lived just across the road from Aunt Tregear, so it was easy for them to come.

Supper was to be laid in the mowey, on long wooden tables from Levant Count House, with Aunt Tregear's best white damask tablecloths to cover them. The girls had been picking fox-gloves and cow-parsley all morning to fill the pitchers for down the centre of each table, and the boys had been puffing and blowing up hill with forms from the Sunday School for people to sit on. What a sight it would be when the food was laid and the lamps alight and all the happy faces around.

It was only a frog's leap from their house to hers, so Grace was agog to go. She had not been too well lately, after her last baby boy, John, was born. It took her a long time to get over the birth, and she still couldn't walk too far. Just right the distance to Aunt Tregear's would be, and the change would do her a world of good. Maddern could carry her back home if needs be; she was as light as a feather. They wouldn't worry about the children being left behind on their own; Mabel was old enough now to look after them for a few hours. If the bedroom window was left open and they sat at the end table underneath it they would hear Mabel call if anything went wrong.

Off they set, just as the sun went down. Grace in her dark blue striped velvet dress, altered a bit since her wedding day. Maddern could span her waist that year: 18 inches it was. He could almost do it now, with a bit of a squeeze and a giggle. A good looking woman she was. Her husband, Maddern, handsome in his Sunday-going-to-Meeting suit, picked a pink rose from above the porch for his buttonhole on his way.

Mabel, Gracie, Willy and little Olive held baby John up to wave good-bye and to watch the pair as they crossed the road to the mowey. They could see the tables, the lamps already alight although it wasn't yet dimsey. Great silver grey moths fluttered against the tapering glass chimleys, battering themselves to death. Gracie felt a little chill near her heart; pisgies (moths) were said to be departed souls. She hoped they stayed where they were down there, and didn't fly up to the bedroom window. Willy nearly fell over the window sill craning his neck to see round the corner of the house who was coming up the hill. Mabel had to hang on to the tail of his night shirt to hold him steady. Mabel felt most important. It was the first time she had been trusted to look after the children. She bossed them around a bit, getting them all to bed by nine. She had learned to tell the time by the church clock opposite.

It was just after the hour when she looked again. She could see the church and the carn above, all pink and gold in the setting sun, and could hear the laughing and talking in the mowey below.

Mabel didn't feel a bit sleepy, and knew Gracie and Willy were wide awake. Baby John was breathing softly; thank goodness he was asleep. What were Gracie and Willy giggling about? She threw a pillow at their heads to stop them making too much noise and waking the baby. This started something going which almost put an end to Aunt Tregear's birthday party.

Maddern and Grace sat where they wanted to, at the end table close to their own house, Grace facing the bedroom window where she hoped the children were fast asleep. Maddern was talking to William Henry about the price of tin and Mary Liz, Grace's sister, sitting next to her, was prattling on about the price of a jug of gin and how much Grandma Oates put away in a week. Someone said what a lovely evening it was. Aunt Tregear said it was getting a bit clammy. It must be the mist coming up the hill from the sea. She had best go and get her mantle. Grace looked across the road at their house to see that everything was alright, but it wasn't mist they could see – it was smoke, billowing out of the bedroom window and drifting across the mowey towards them in the twilight.

"Maddern! Quick!" she screeched, "the house is on fire."

Mary Liz was off like a streak of lightning, through the gap in the hedge and across the road, Maddern after her, jumping the gate. Grace was last, puffing and panting down the path. It wasn't smoke she could see, more like snow flakes falling all around her. Through the gate her feet didn't touch the ground, up the path, through the epps and up the stairs. Maddern, Grace and Mary Liz burst open the door of the bedroom. They couldn't see across the room for swirling, twirling goose feathers.

"Johnny, Johnny, my baby boy. Where are you my handsome?"

Grace was beside herself. She must get to the cradle first, but Maddern was there before her and lifted his son free of his little white cot. Mabel tried to hide under what was left of the bolster, Gracie peeped out from the tye and Willy hid under the bed.

"I'll warm your bottoms for you!" Mary Liz shrieked, taking up Grandpa's old black umbrella from behind the washing stand.

"Get your slippers on and down the stairs you go, you varmets. You've spoilt the evening for your Ma and Pa."

Bedlam broke loose, Bessie the dog howling, children screaming, baby John screeching at the top of his lungs and Mary Liz beating the saucepans, hanging on the beams of the kitchen ceiling, with Grandpa's old gamp to stop the racket.

So much noise went on that Maddern and Grace slipped out of the back door and returned to the party, too relieved to be angry.

Mary Liz was left in the kitchen with the children. She didn't know where to turn; the goose feathers were sticking to everything. Baby John looked like a little fledgling owl, peeping from his make-shift cot of a drawer from the dresser.

It seemed like hours afterwards. The children had been cleaned up and were sitting in front of the slab's open doors, drinking hot milk and sugar. Mary Liz had a drop of gin in her tea. Everyone had a good laugh and vowed they had never been to such a good birthday party before.

THE LITTLE PRIVY.

CHAPTER FOUR

HAPPENINGS AND FOREBODINGS

IT WAS Christmas Eve. Mary Liz stirred the fire, putting the poker between the bars of the slab and shoving it to and fro. It left a huge glowing hole in the middle of the coals. She didn't like the look of this at all; it meant a death in the family. She lifted the heavy iron fountain and put it on the ring above the flames to boil. Mother would need hot water for her stone bottle which was warming on the fender – and a drop to put in her nightcap to warm her in bed, inside as well as out.

Mary Liz was tired after a heavy day. She was in the shop much more now that Oggy Diddle had gone and Lizzy Tish was getting near to the end of her time. Silly Lizzy – whatever had she got messed up with that old thing for? That old thing was old enough to be her father, and she was old enough to know better. Still, she was going to have the baby. She was braver than some of the girls of her age who got into trouble. Most of them made their way up the hill to Nanny Ninepins' cottage as soon as they knew, and had the little thing wished away. Or worse still, some didn't seem to know until it was too late. Then it had to be born in secret and sneaked down the garden path at the dead of night, after decent people were abed, to the little privy amongst the rhubarb and stinging nettles.

Some old farmers said pee was good for rhubarb. Mary Liz could remember she and her brother were always sent down the back garden by the wall to wee on the rhubarb instead of using the privy. It was alright for William Henry, but she had a dreadful time pulling her drawers down, trying to avoid the nettles stinging her bottom. True, there were always docks growing nearby, and well she knew the chant: "dock leaf go in, stingnettle go out," but it wasn't the easiest spot to rub, and one couldn't shout for someone else to do it.

Going back in her mind to Lizzy Tish and Oggy Diddle, it was the best way in the world to get rid of a poor unwanted mite; to meet daft old Grumbler Quilken behind the overgrown closet after dark who would wrap the little thing up carefully in his apron and take it across Woon Gumpas Common and over the moors to Madron Workhouse, with nobody the wiser.

It was Christmas Eve. The wind was blowing in from the sea, slithering around the house and up the valley. A storm was brewing; Mary Liz could feel it in her bones. Her big toe had been jumping all day; this was always a sure sign of rain. The horses and cattle on the cliff tops would have fitty shelter tonight. Mary Liz remembered her grand-father telling her at bed time that all the animals

GRUMBLER QUILKEN.

knelt down in the fields as the clock struck twelve on Christmas Eve, when our Lord was born in Bethlehem. Would they kneel tonight, she wondered, among the bracken below the sheltering granite hedges. A good man her grandfather was; a church warden up at St. John's until the day he drowned. What a Christmas Eve that was. Never had such a storm got up so quickly, or lasted so long. Three days and three nights! People do say the spray came up so high that it tarnished the face of the church clock.

Mary Liz's two uncles, Edwin and Samuel, perished with Grandpa. Edwin was walking out with a girl from Penzance, and Samuel was engaged to a girl from St. Day. Samuel used to go courting once a month, taking a day to go and a day to come back, with a day in between for a bit of hanky-panky. That particular Christmas Eve Grandpa and the two young men went off to Portherris beach bright and early for a morning's fishing. A few pilchards for marinating didn't seem worth it, somehow, but Grandma wanted her favourite Christmas supper, and what Grandma wanted she usually had . . . Three men drowned; three lives thrown away!

Grandma never got over it, she just sat by the fire in winter and in the sun porch in the summer and wasted away. Mary Liz's mother said that the old black ravens croaked above the house for days before the drowning happened.

Mary Liz hated superstitions. She thought it was a sort of fear-like religion that the old people had. Her mother was almost afraid to do anything. Mary Liz had been brought up this way. Her mother laid the law down as to what they could do and what they couldn't do for fear of the consequences – such as saying "Good morrow, Brother" to one magpie to ease the bad luck, not seeing the new moon through glass, musn't pass anyone on the stairs, or enter a house by one door and leave by another. Her mother wouldn't wear green, or put her hat on a table, or open an umbrella indoors, nor would she take off anything she had put on first thing in the morning. "Bad luck to change it" she would say. Mary Liz could feel even now the discomfort of wearing combinations back-to-front all day. In fact, she would often sneak out to the wash-house and change them when her mother wasn't looking. As for the forbidden wildflowers such as May blossom, bluebells, heather and cowslips that children like to pick from the lanes to bring home for Mothering Sunday, she wouldn't have them in the house.

"Take them out" she would say if Mary Liz or her brother and sisters brought little hot-handed bunches of flowers to her. "Can't abide them, throw them over the hedge. I know you meant well, but they will bring us bad luck before the Summer's through."

Mary Liz remembered one May Day especially. It was the custom for children to rise very early on the 1st of May to a-Maying. They would roam the countryside singing, dancing, blowing horns and making merry while gathering May blossom to decorate the doorways and window-sills of their homes – home where bowls of junket and cream would be a-waiting their return. There was one May tree in particular on the Carn that looked a picture, laden with blossom and bowing low to the ground as most thorn trees do in

PORTHERRAS COVE.

Penwith. Mary Liz didn't know then that it was the salt in the air from the sea and not the prevailing west wind that caused their misshapen boughs. Her brother, Johnny, helped cut the scratchy branches with his penknife. With arm-fuls of blossom home they skipped thinking their mother would be delighted with this lucky gift. She was, however, horrified.

From then on things didn't go at all well. Mother was teasy all day. Her favourite cat, Fishy, fell down the well outside the back door. Johnny fell in head first trying to get it up in a bucket and Mr. Penwarden next door had to jump down nearly ten feet to rescue both of them. Poor man, he died the very next day from catching cold, and his wife the day after that from missing him.

Mary Liz and Johnny were deeply shocked. Had they caused all the trouble and confusion because of their gift of the branches from the little May tree?

Mary Liz used to clap her hands over her ears as a young girl, so as not to hear a robin sweetly singing. "'Tis bad news on its way." Granny would say and she would sit by the window waiting for it to happen. As for a bird pecking at the pane – tap, tap, tap, tck, tck, that was worst of all.

Mary Liz looked over at the window. It was almost dimsey outside and beginning to sleet a bit. Tap, tap, tap – a little jenny wren was knocking at the glass pane. Mary Liz crossed the kitchen and swished the curtains closed.

"Go away, little bird. Go away, we want no ill news tonight. 'Tis a good job Ma can't hear you. She would be up half the night waiting for the tap, tap, tap at the door."

CHAPTER FIVE

THE GOOSE AND THE GREENS

GRACE TREMBATH was not looking forward to Christmas. Maddern had been, it seemed forever, away in Africa. He'd gone with the rest of them, in the mad rush for gold. His last words before he left were: "You'll be able to follow soon with the children. It won't be long to wait, Grace, only till I make the fare for the passage."

But, in his last letter, things didn't seem too good. Bloomfontaine, where he was, was only a shanty town, and what with the heat and sickness about he didn't seem so keen for them to join him for a while.

Grace worried too much. She knew this. It was all very well for Dinah, her cousin, to say "it will be alright in the end." Grace felt she must make a specially good Christmas for the children this year so she got a chair and stood on it to put the star on top of the holly tree. She'd done her best. There was a good sized goose in the larder, with mince pies, cream and saffron cake. Upstairs, hanging in her wardrobe, were two little suits and three little coats in olive green velvet, with swandown trimmings for the girls and brass buttons for the boys that Mrs. Rescorla had made for the children to wear to church. Mary Liz and Dinah were going to take the children to church whilst Grace cooked the dinner. Grandma Oates and Annie Jane, her other daughter, were going to

join them for the day. They would miss the men folk, but they had got Willy and Johnny.

Grace went to the door to see if it was snowing yet. It was cold enough and dark enough. The sky over the Carn was blue-black. Against the skyline, startling black and white, a magpie teetered on the gate post.

"Good morrow, Brother" said Grace, shutting the door as quickly as she could. She didn't like seeing one magpie at this time of day. No light left to look out of the window to see if it had a mate.

"One for sorrow,
Two for mirth,
Three for a marriage,
Four for a birth,
Five for something new,
Six for something old and
Seven for a secret that's never been told."

Grace chanted as she went up to bed. Little did she know what news the bird of ill omen would bring on the morrow.

Next morning, Grace laid the table in the kitchen before the sun was up. She had a lot to do this Christmas day. If only Maddern were here to help.

CREAN WOODS.

The kitchen door into the hall was open and she could see the holly tree, with its star on top, standing in the corner of the parlour, groaning with gifts and tinsel. The shiny balls were brought home from Paris by Cap'n Denley. He would be wed to her cousin in Penzance before the year was out.

She watched the first rays of the morning sun streaming through the door. A pretty glass door it was, with panes of crimson, gold and green, with a mauve and silver lily flower in the centre, just like the north window up at the church. The colours were reflected across the tiled floor and up the wall. Grace thought she heard the door open very softly – was it someone creeping across the hall and up the creaking stairs? Maddern used to tip-toe like that when he came home late from the North Inn on a Saturday night so as not to wake the baby.

Grace paused in folding the table cloth. Why was she thinking so much about her husband today? Perhaps it was because of the magpie she saw last thing. She was getting worse than her mother. These silly old superstitions were only hearsay. She felt chilly and turned to poke the fire.

There was a swishing noise above the house. The starlings were on their way over to Creen Woods to feed. Or was it another sound? The wind, maybe . . . but there was no wind. Her ears were playing her tricks. Best she got on with the dinner; she still had the taties and sprouts to do. The children would be down in a minute. She could hear their excited voices as they opened their stockings in the bedroom above. Now that she had laid the table for dinner they would have to eat their porridge on their laps by the fire before they went to church. Mary Liz would be here soon to collect them. Dinah, Annie May and Grandma Oates, all decked out in their Sunday best, would follow later.

She bustled about doing little nothings to keep her mind busy so as not to think of other Christmases when they were last all together as a family.

Grace was just taking the goose out of the oven to baste when there was a banging at the back door. Who on earth was come now? she wondered. Maybe Mrs. Corin from next door to borrow a drop of milk. But when she opened the door it was young Jimmy White's boy, red in the face from running.

"Missus Trembath, Missus Trembath!" – he could hardly get his words out – "Ther's a man down at the mine looking for you. He's come all the way from St. Just – in an awful state he is and his horse is all covered with lather."

Grace could see the stranger coming up the road. She rushed out of the door and down the path to meet him, her pinny flying in the wind. She could see by his face something was wrong.

"You be Missus Grace Trembath?" he asked.

"Yes" gasped Grace.

"I ain't got very good news for 'ee Missus. Your husband be Maddern Trembath of Pendeen, Cornwall, now working in Bloomfontaine, South Africa?"

"Yes." Grace felt her heart fall down to her feet.

"Well, I don't know how to tell 'ee, m'dear, but – poor man – he be dead. Cap'n White had news by telegram first thing this morning. I came as quick as my 'oss could carry me to tell 'ee. He died of fever, nursing a friend in the camp who had the same disease."

Grace had felt all morning something was wrong and now she knew. Her life had come to an end, here on Christmas day in Pendeen on her very own doorstep. She tried to speak; no words came. She put her apron over her head and sat down on the porch step. The man looked to go away. She must pull herself together and call him back. Thank God the children were still in church and Grandma up in the kitchen having her tot of gin

from the little leather and pewter covered bottle she kept in her pinny pocket.

"Please Mister," at last her voice came back. "Come inside. You must be dead tired and need a glass of something or a morsel to eat."

The mince pies were on top of the slab, warming. She kept only a little brandy in the top dresser cupboard for anyone feeling faint. They didn't keep much drink in the house now Maddern was away. Away! He would never come back again to need it now. "Maddern, oh Maddern, why ever did you go away and leave us?" Poor Grace was overcome.

Mary Liz, coming in the door, gathered something was wrong. She pushed the children into the parlour with Dinah, hissing in her ear to keep them there, to open their presents under the holly tree.

She pulled Grace across the room, sat her down in the rocking chair by the fire and signalled the strange man to the settle opposite, trying hard all the time to think where the brandy was kept. She put the kettle on, made some tea and put a good drop of brandy in each cup. She had found the bottle on top of the dresser, up away from the children. By now Grace had a bit of colour in her face and Mr. Tonkin, as the man was called, looked a bit better.

Mary Liz had to think fast. The best thing she could do was to carry on as usual. Grace would cope as best she could. Mary Liz knew her sister well enough for that. Grandma Oates would sleep most of the afternoon after her dinner. Dinner! The goose! She looked in the oven. The bird was cooked, so dinner was served up on the plates. The children, hungry and excited, chatted like magpies. She asked Mr. Tonkin to stay, but he shook his head, saying his turkey was waiting for him at home.

After the goose the plum pudding, then the fruit and nuts. Then tea and Christmas cake and mince pies and seedy biscuits. So it went on.

The four grown-ups kept going until nightfall. People came and went. All the village knew by now. They felt the sorrow that Grace felt and tried to share it with her. When midnight came Grace shut the door on her family and Uncle John, her last visitor. She could not sleep and did not want to go to bed, so she sat in the rocking chair. Mary Liz had built up the fire last thing before she left and Uncle John had poured out the last of the brandy saying – drink it down, my gold, it will do you the world of good.

What was she going to do? Four little children left without their father. Had Maddern come back that morning? she wondered, to see them all just once again? Would she ever get over it?

Grace Trembath did get over it in time. Things were not too easy for her at first. The family as ever was divided. Maddern's father and Great Aunt Trembath wanted to take young Gracie and Willy to live on the other side of Pendeen with them. Grandma Oates wanted Mabel and Olive to live in the Square with her. But Grace couldn't split up her family. She did not want to live in the house by the church any more. There were too many memories under its roof. Anyway, she had little money to live on. Maddern Trembath was only thirty-two when he died. He had lived a good life, but not saved money.

The feud between the two families did not mend because of the tragedy; it seemed to be much worse, with one thing and another, so Grace packed her bags and took her family into Penzance to start a business in Alverton.

So began a new phase in her life, but a goose at Christmas and the wearing of green became a family superstition.

PENDEEN CHURCH GATEWAY.

CHAPTER SIX

A SUMMER'S WEDDING

WILLIAM OATÉ and Mary Jane Oates were married in June at the new church on the hill at Pendeen. The couple were very well liked. Friends came from all over West Penwith; some left home before sunrise to be with them on that happy day. Villagers said afterwards the horses and carriages stretched down the hill all the way to Tregaseal. The church had an ironwork gateway by the front steps. All the Sunday School children had decorated it with foxgloves, bluebells and cow parsley.

Mary Jane wore a white grosgrain crinoline with sky-blue velvet bows (true lovers' knots) around the hem, and forget-me-nots in her bonnet to match her eyes. Her two sisters were bridesmaids in magenta taffeta, and carried foxgloves and ragged robin. Dear Miss Scobey came over from St. Just for three weeks before the wedding day to sew the dresses. The patterns came all the way from Paris, and some of the young girls from the parish helped with the buttonholes, seams and hemming, working all day by hand.

Many a titbit of gossip passed between them as they sat sewing in the spare room. Miss Scobey could tell a good yarn when she got going, and the girls squiggled and squirmed in their seats when they guessed whom she was talking about.

The best one was about Mrs. Carbines and the pixie-led needle. Carrie Carbines was Miss Scobey's pupil apprentice. She was sewing one day in her small dark room when she lost her needle; she had a habit of putting it in her mouth when she was gathering or pleating. A candle was brought and the whole family went down on their hands and knees looking for it. Her poor husband, who was only a little man, had to lift the wardrobe to see if it was underneath. They searched till tea-time, but no needle could be found. Poor Carrie was beside herself. Her husband tried to pacify her, but all she could say was that she had swallowed the needle. "Oh deary, deary me, what shall I do?"

Months went by. Carrie gave up sewing and just sat around all day feeling poorly. In the end she took to her bed and wouldn't see anybody. The new doctor was called from St. Just, and a specialist from Truro. Neither of them could find any evidence that the needle was inside her, but Carrie knew it was.

By now her husband was at his wit's end. His mother suggested that he consult an old woman who lived in Pengersick who had cured many local people of very odd things. One woman his mother knew, Minnie Mumchance, thought that she, Minnie Mumchance, was in the family way,

brother was boiling up kettles of water, and the steam was streaming out of the cottage windows. Minnie was up in bed shouting; "Quick, quick! Send for Nanny Ninepins, the baby's nearly here!"

The old woman went up the stairs, told Minnie to hold on and gave her a very strong cup of herby tea, saying it would ease things a bit. It did. Minnie became quite quiet and went off to sleep in no time. The old woman made all the preparations that were usual in childbirth, even to tying Minnie's feet to the bedpost, and then went off downstairs to have a cup of tea with the brother.

About three hours after, the old woman took the piglet out of her brown bag, dressed it in the bonnet and shawl and took it upstairs. The piglet had also had a drop of herby tea, but the effect was wearing off and it began to screech like a Witnick. Minnie was also waking up; she saw all the array around her and started to cry.

"Never mind, my dear," the old woman said, "it's all over now. Here's your dear little newborn baby. Hold out your arms, the poor little mite is hungry."

She put the warm bundle into Minnie's lap. Poor woman, she let out a dreadful howl.

"Take it away, give it away. It's not a baby, it's some awful creater. However did I get myself into this sort of mess? I don't want to see it ever again."

The old woman did as she was bid. Next day Minnie was up and about her business; she paid the old woman her due, arranged for the funeral, saw the undertaker and the parson. Three days later they followed the little coffin up the churchyard path. The old woman followed with her heavy

although she'd never been near a man. Poor soul, it was all in her mind. She even had pains in her stomach and early morning sickness. She lived down Botallack way with her brother, who was also at his wit's end to know what to do with her. In the end, the old woman from Pengersick was called. On her way to Botallack she collected one or two things to bring with her; wild herbs from the hedges, a newly born piglet from farmer Trezise and a shawl and bonnet from his wife.

When the old woman arrived she could hear the racket going on from up the lane. Minnie's brown bag well tied up with string and two holes in the bottom. "It's all in the mind," she muttered as she went up the lane on the way to return the contents to the farmer and his wife. Then, home to Pengersick.

So Carrie Carbine's husband called for the old woman from Pengersick. She came as soon as she could with the same brown bag on her arm and a large black umbrella. She went upstairs, spent a long time with Carrie, then came downstairs again with a needle in her hand.

"'Tis found" she said, "Poor Carrie, it worked its way down through her body and popped right out of her big toe."

Carrie followed her into the room, a bit weak, but all smiles.

CARRIE CARBINE'S COTTAGE.

"I knew I was right," she said, "I had swallowed the needle."

Carrie's husband was astounded but greatly relieved. He gave the old woman toad-in-the-hole and gooseberry wine for her supper. He carried his wife up to her bed and she was soon sound asleep. Downstairs again, he asked the visitor one question,

"How did you find it?"

"'Twas easy. Poor soul, it was all in her mind as I expected. I just pinched her toe till the tears came to her eyes, then showed her the needle which I brought along with me in my little brown bag. Don't you ever let on," she warned, "she must never know the truth."

Next morning she left for Pengersick. Carrie was never the wiser.

Miss Scobey finished her story and bade the village girls go home to their beds.

The Oates had a lovely walled garden at the back of their house. After the wedding service their friends and relatives gathered there for a luncheon party. The tables were laden with cold hams and rabbit pies, pickles and home-made chutney with strawberries and cream to follow. There was enough cider, elderberry wine and Grandpa Oates' sloe gin to sink a ship. Everyone drank the couple's health and happiness.

The celebrations lasted all day till well on into the evening. The sun had sunk into the sea before the last carriage drove away. William and Mary Jane left early as they had a long journey to Penzance to catch the railway train to Plymouth for their honeymoon.

MANY A TITBIT OF GOSSIP.

CHAPTER SEVEN

EARLY DAYS AT ST. DAY

WILLIAM and Mary Jane Oaté's marriage started off with a big disappointment.

William was building a house for his new bride on top of the hill above Trewellard. It had a fine position along from the main road and a splendid view across the Atlantic; one could see the Scilly Islands on a clear day. Mind you, there weren't so many clear days up on the North Road. The mist had a way of sneaking up from the cliffs when you least expected it. Pixie mist swirled and whirled round the mine stacks and down soot laden cottage chimleys to make the black cats on the hearth rug even blacker. The house had taken longer to finish than William expected. The stone, quarried from Carn Eanes, had been used in finishing the new church, so fresh stone had to be broken and cut for his walls and foundations. William's father was a master builder and designer of mine buildings. He had constructed the air vent on the top of Cape Cornwall, and helped with most engine houses from the Crown Mines to Wheal Geevor. William's brother, Charles, hated the tin mines and the rough barren country around them as much as William loved it all. Charles was older than William and the following story was always told amongst the family when reminiscing, especially by their father, over glasses of brandy and treacle in The North Inn.

Old man Oaté and Charles were repairing a chimley stack above the cliffs west of Botallack. A storm was brewing; they could see the birds circling around their heads, which was a sure sign of bad weather. The wind was already blowing the creamy spume up the cliff side, catching in the heather and gorse as it flew towards them. It caught in Charles' hair, and the spray stung his face. His hands were freezing. The spume clung to his beard like froth on a pint of ale which, as he wiped it off, reminded him and made him long for The North Inn and its warm and snug bar parlour. He was passing up bricks in a pail on a rope to his father who clung above him on top of a

ST. DAY CHURCH.

ladder. Suddenly he felt he could no longer carry on. "Father," he shouted against the wind. "Dammy, I'm bloddy well fed up and sick of all this." Throwing his trowel over the cliff he went home to Pendeen, and left for America within the month. William missed his brother, he could have done with his help in the evenings building the house!

Charles had a tragic life in the New World. He did well in his exams and became an architect in good time, but his life ended all too soon. He was killed travelling in a carriage and pair which overturned in a busy city street. Afterwards, a plan for the city's new cathedral was found in his pocket.

William knew now that it would take a year for his house to be completed, so he had to find a home for his new bride as soon as their honeymoon was over. A temporary home, but where? William racked his brains. With Grandpa Oates and Grandma? No room; the old people had moved into a smaller cottage down the hill. His father? No, he had become a saddened man since Charles had died in America. Mary Jane's family? He didn't think he could face it. They were good enough in their way, but William couldn't imagine living all day long among a parcel of women chatting away like magpies in a hawthorn tree. He went to ask his aunt Bessie. She looked at him with a smile in her eyes when he told her about facing the parcel of women.

"Well," she said, "there's your father's brother, Joseph, over at St. Day. He used to have a cottage a field away from his farm. His herdsman lived there. I think he has moved further down the valley nearer Ponsanooth, so it must be empty. I should think Uncle Joseph would oblige you and Mary Jane."

He did, and they moved to St. Day early in July. William could find plenty of work with so many mines in the district. The cottage was old and a bit damp in the corner of the kitchen and bedroom above. William could easily cure that with a bucket of lime and some cow dung. He'd seen his father do it many a time. He decided to go ahead of Mary Jane; there were a few other things to do. She arrived some days later with a wagon load of furniture and their luggage. A proper sight she felt as she stepped down into the waiting arms of William, what with her bonnet all askew and her hair blown all over the place. William didn't mind; he was so pleased to see her. He carried her over the threshold as all good bridegrooms do.

Inside, the room was softly lighted and the fire roared up the chimney, but there seemed to be – Mary Jane couldn't quite put her finger on it – a sort of chill around her. She must be very tired. It had been a long journey. She had left Pendeen at five o'clock that morning. She was very hungry as well, so they sat down right away to cold rabbit pie which her mother had sent with her and some sloe gin William had found in the corner cupboard. It was a merry meal, the sloe gin smelled a bit funny but tasted alright. They finished every crumb of the pie and emptied the bottle.

William knew Mary Jane was very tired, so he damped down the fire and lighted her candle for bed. As she mounted the stairs Mary Jane looked up. There was an odd swishing sound above her head. The candle flame fluttered and went out. She felt trembly and very queer inside so she sat down on the stair. William stood at the bottom and roared with laughter.

"You've had too much tiddley, Mary Jane."

He ran up the stairs, scooped her up in his arms and carried her off to bed.

July was a very hot month. Mary Jane and William spent most of their spare time in the garden cleaning the flower-beds of brambles, and raking and hoeing the gravel paths which were bordered with honeysuckle hedges that had to be clipped into shape. William fancied planting daphne bushes along under the parlour window. The flowers smelled so sweetly. His father had told him the way to plant daphne was to split the stem of the cutting and put a grain of corn between the two halves. He bought some corn from the miller, and Uncle Joseph gave him the cuttings. He hoped by the time they left St. Day he would have strong leaved bushes from them to plant in a sheltered spot in Pendeen. It was so exposed down there that only montbretia, marigolds and sweet william did well. Here in St. Day roses and lilies filled the air with their sweet scent and the cottage gardens were a blaze of colour.

As August went into September the evenings grew darker and longer, so they had to spend more time indoors. Sitting by the fire, their puppy dog, Bess, beside them, they planned their future home. William was carving a stool for Mary Jane's feet to rest on, and Mary Jane started sewing a patchwork quilt. She had collected bits and pieces from all her friends' wedding gowns to start the centre and make up the border pattern.

One Sunday night a storm blew up. They could hear it above in the trees and whining down

the chimley. It was just like back home at Pendeen. When the wind blew there the houses shook, and so much racket went on you couldn't hear yourself speak. William drew the curtain at the bottom of the stair; it was a draughty old parlour at the best of times. The curtain billowed out even now, so he pulled the settle right across in front of the fire, and they ate their supper in comfort.

About eight the wind passed over and left the lamp-lit room very still. Mary Jane felt the odd feeling inside her again. The puppy shuddered and ran whimpering under the dresser from where she watched something moving around the room, her little head going from side to side as she followed with her eyes whatever it was. That same swishing sound went over their heads, the flame in the lamp went down and up again and the candle on the dresser spluttered and went out. The curtain at the bottom of the stair blew out so much that it fell from the rod, the brass rings clattering all over the floor.

"Whatever is it, William?" Mary Jane said.

"I don't know," he replied, "'t'is very odd and no mistake. The wind went down an hour ago, all the windows were closed upstairs and the back and front doors were bolted last thing."

From there on till the time they left William, and especially Mary Jane, had no peace. Quite large objects, like the brass candlestick on the dresser, flung themselves across the kitchen. William's slippers seemed to be possessed; they were never in the same place. If he had put them by the slab he found them in the larder. If he left them upstairs they somehow came downstairs. Jugs fell off their hooks, plates rolled off the table and one of a pair of china dogs, the one with the wall eye, fell off the mantlepiece. They had been a wedding present from Uncle William. Mary Jane was very fond of them and of Uncle William, but worst of all was Mary Jane's beloved sailor boy. He seemed to jump off the corner cupboard and smash to smithereens on the slate floor. Something happened to them every day. The poor puppy lived in fear of her life. She wouldn't sleep downstairs. The only place she semed happy was on the end of their bed, so they let her sleep between them.

It got so bad that in the end it affected Mary Jane's health, so William packed their bags, carefully wrapping his daphne cuttings in balls of earth, put a collar and lead on the puppy and left the herdsman's cottage for good, to return to Pendeen to live with Mary Jane's mother, parcel of women and all, 'till the new home was ready.

CHAPTER EIGHT

GREAT GRANDPA'S DAUGHTER'S CURE

WILLIAM OATÉ and Mary Jane went into their new house on top of the hill above Trewellard on the 24th March. It was stout and strong to stand against all the winds that blow. Alongside the back kitchen wall was a linny with a small high window; it was always a little ajar. Each night Mary Jane left on the window shelf a saucer of milk for the pixie to find. When he came she never knew, but first thing in the morning the saucer was empty. Her mother had always done this, and her grandmother before her. Mary Jane could remember, as a child, standing on a chair for ages in the linny to see if the pixie came back in the daylight, but he never did. Her father used to laugh and say it was someone's cat, but she had been outside in the field to see; the little window was far too high for any cat to climb up the wall and enter.

In the front of the house, over the main door, William had built a glass porch with square coloured panes, greengage green, crimson pink and plum purple. It was a pretty sight on a summer's evening to sit and watch the play of colour on Mary Jane's head bent over her patch-work.

They were very happy; Mary Jane was expecting. Her first piece of patchwork was finished and made into a quilt for their mahogany

bed upstairs in the bedroom. The bedroom was very pretty. William and his father had made a whole mahogany suite. The bed had a carved head-board inset with a paisley pleated curtain. The dressing table had an oval mirror with three little drawers each side and curved legs. The washing stand was made to match, with a white marble top from Carrara, Italy.

Aunt Bessie had given them the jug and basin and its accessories for a wedding present – white and mauve porcelain with bunches of purple violets and rose pink bows. The linoleum was a new idea. Mary Jane didn't like it very much, it was cold to the feet first thing in the morning, so she had put down Grandma's rag rugs by the bedside. They were colourful, and somehow went well with the patchwork quilt. The wallpaper was Mary Jane's delight: striped pink satin with bunches of violets dotted here and there. With lace curtains at the two windows it was a fitty place in which to sleep.

Now she was making another quilt for the new baby's cot.

William was planning the garden in front of the house. He had built a wall on the north-east side to shelter the flowers in the beds. His daphne cuttings from St. Day were doing well under the window by the front door. He had planted sycamores around the west side; they didn't mind the salt in the air. It would be good if they grew because there wasn't a tree in sight. He hoped to have vegetables in the back garden, taties and cabbage, no broccoli; broccoli didn't grow well in small patches, they were big field plants. He had a mowey at the south side. He hoped to keep a cow and a pig or two. Mary Jane fancied a few hens. Maybe, in a few years to come, a pony for the expected little one to ride.

William hoped Mary Jane would be alright. Her time was nearly come and she was such a frail little thing.

Mary Jane's baby did come, much earlier than expected. She was three days in labour; if it wasn't for Mother Roscorla she would have died; the poor soul was twisted and torn, but the baby was fine. Plump and pink with masses of black curly hair and big brown eyes. She grew strong and handsome, as did the sister and two brothers after her. Mary Jane had four children in five years: Dinah, Lizzy Annie, William Joseph and Charley.

The sycamore trees grew a bit stunted but they held their own, and the daphne bushes scented the summer evenings. There were two cows and a calf, four pigs and twenty hens, milk, butter, cream and eggs for all of them and plenty of fresh vegetables to eat, and still some left to give away. Sometimes Mary Jane felt afraid. They were all so happy, strong and healthy.

William had taken over the business from his father who had retired to live with his daughter. There was plenty of work for builders; many miners had found gold in Africa, Australia and America and had come back to Cornwall to buy land and build large houses for their families to live in. He was making money and doing well. Mary Jane felt much stronger these days. She loved being alive, but the little fear grew in her heart. It was all too good to be true.

Then, one summer's day, what she feared happened. Dinah fell sick. Not to notice at first; in fact they used to laugh at her and call her butter-fingers. She started to drop things, such as a cup of milk or her school books or the china candlestick she took to bed. They soon became sorry that they had laughed. She grew thin and weak; all her dresses had to be taken in; her tiny hands became listless and she could walk only a few steps at a time supported by her brother and sister. Her father would carry her down to see his family, and whenever Mary Jane went to see her mother and sisters who lived further away she would be pushed in a sort of go-cart William had designed. They tried every doctor and specialist in Penwith and Cornwall, but all the medicines and exercises that were prescribed made little difference. Dinah was wasting away before their very eyes.

William did again what he had done when they were first married; he went to see Aunt Bessie. She greeted him with the same smile in her eye and said almost the same things she had said before.

"Ther's your father's brother's herdsman at St. Day. He's done wonders for cattle, and menfolk as well. Some say he is the wisest man in Cornwall."

William, after a cup of tea and a saffron bun and a peep at Aunt Bessie's new litter of puppies, made his way homewards with a heavy heart. He knew Mary Jane would never go back to St. Day and, although she believed in pixies, she couldn't abide anything to do with witchcraft, whether it was good or bad. After the odd things that had happened in the cottage at St. Day, who could blame her? Maybe that's why she gave the pixies milk – to pacify them. William knew she put a lump of sugar in the saucer of milk on the sly for a treat every Sunday when no-one was looking. Mary Jane would never go to see a herdsman about Dinah; he knew that as he put his foot over the doorstep and he was right. She did put her foot down. No daughter of hers was going to be handled by a herdsman, not over her dead body. No, no, no. If the good Lord meant Dinah to die die she would, and no-one could stop it.

Dinah took to her bed and lost interest in almost everything. Mary Jane sitting by her daughter's bedside one afternoon, looked out of the bedroom window at the blue sky and sunlit sea, the waves dancing merrily away to the islands of Scilly. Somewhere, deep down inside her, she knew she must give up her selfish feelings and let Dinah have a chance to be cured, even in an unnatural way, if this were possible. There was a big doubt in Mary Jane's mind. There was doubt in William's mind as well, but he was overjoyed that Mary Jane had at last agreed, so word was sent to Ponsanooth.

The drive to St. Day would take three days in comfort. One day on the way, spending the night with Aunt Bessie's brother, then one day to see the herdsman at Ponsanooth, back for the night with uncle Joseph, then home again the next morning.

They set off early. The sun was shining. It was a lovely day and Mary Jane was glad William was so happy. She, herself, tried to appear brave, but underneath she was very frightened. It was their last chance to save Dinah's life. The doctors all said alike: by Christmas she would have wasted away and be dead. How the illness had occurred, none of them could say. Some said it was passed on from someone in the family of an earlier generation. Both William and Mary Jane racked their brains, but could not think of such an illness or person in their family. Others said it was in the very ground they stood on – poison in the granite rocks around them. Poison in the blood was another opinion. Mary Jane could not understand how a herdsman who cured cattle could possibly help her daughter to get better.

They arrived at the man's cottage just before noon. He was waiting for them, smoking a clay pipe, sitting on an old tree trunk outside his gate. He wasn't an old wizened man as they had expected. He was big and burly with eyes of a different colour – one blue eye to look up to heaven and one brown eye to look down to earth. A shock of red hair and curly beard surrounded his face. He smiled at Mary Jane and took her by the arm to help her down from the trap.

"You must be Mrs. Oaté who has the sick child down at Pendeen," he said.

Aunt Bessie had told them not to say anything to the herdsman without he asked them a definite question. Also, they must not thank him or offer him any money.

"Come on in," he said "and have a glass of blackberry wine. I make it myself. It's very good when one feels a bit down."

They sat in the garden on a bench by the front door. William noticed how many herbs there were growing between the pansies, marigold and mignonette. The men discussed plants and cattle over their pipes. Mary Jane sipped her wine feeling a bit sleepy. They talked on and on about everything under the sun, but not a word about Dinah and her sickness. Just as Mary Jane was about to nod off, the herdsman suddenly stood up and said he must hurry down the Norway valley below Ponsanooth as a horse had falling sickness through eating ragwort. They both knew this was deadly for horses. Mary Jane had heard her Grandpa say witches used ragwort stalks to ride the sky at night. This plant had most unpleasant associations.

He ushered them down the path and through the gate and helped Mary Jane up the steps of the trap. William looked at Mary Jane and Mary Jane looked at William. The herdsman looked at their horse. He gave it a smart slap and away they went at a fair old pace. Just as they turned out of the lane onto the road back to St. Day the herdsman came galloping up on his piebald horse.

"Don't ee worry," he shouted as he passed them, "everything will be alright."

He turned around and galloped off down the valley to Ponsanooth.

JOE

"He is a very strange man" William said. "We shall see what we shall see."

Mary Jane nodded.

They had a lot to talk about to their Uncle Joseph when they got back to his farm. The moon was well up in the sky before they got to bed.

Next day they were up early. The moon was

still in the sky when they thanked Uncle Joseph and rode away. They stopped in Helston to see a cousin, and again in Penzance to pick up some pig food. Then on up the St. Just road and along North Road, the pony now a bit tired but glad to be trotting on the last few miles. Carn Kenidjack was standing out against the evening sky. No wonder the old folk called it "Five Old Hats." This was just what it looked like.

They turned in off the road and rounded the corner. They could see the chimleys smoking and their dog Tuzzy – one of Bessie's puppies – sitting by the gate waiting for them.

Coming up the hill they saw two children carrying a bucket of water between them.

"Look William, ther's young William Joseph and Lizzy Annie. They have been down to the well."

As they got nearer still, Mary Jane could see the little girl had black hair. Lizzy Annie's hair was very fair. It must be Milly down the road helping Joseph. But nearer still, Mary Jane let out a squeal of astonishment.

"William! William! It's Dinah, my Dinah!" she cried – and it was. William could hardly believe his eyes. His little daughter was trudging up the hill, her cheeks flushed and her eyes shining. Her brother was so excited he could hardly speak.

"We've done it, we've done it, Father!" he said. "Lizzy Annie and Aunt Bessie bet that we couldn't, but we have. We've carried the bucket between us all the way."

Mary Jane and William were out and down from the trap in a flash. They were all hugging and kissing each other, the dog going round in circles after his own tail to show his approval. Aunt Bessie who had been looking after the children whilst they were away joined in as well.

"It was unbelievable," she said. "Yesterday Dinah was proper poorly when she woke up, but by mid-day she was sitting up in bed demanding bread and milk with plenty of sugar. But you must be starved and dead tired too. Come on in, supper's all ready."

Afterwards, when the children were asleep and the pony in his stable, Aunt bessie told them how it all happened, how, yesterday afternoon, after her bowl of bread and milk, Dinah had trotted downstairs for a bit of buttered saffron cake for her dinner and a mug of herby beer. Bessie was surprised to see she ate and drank it all and looked for more. Then she asked for a brush and comb, and tidied her hair. From there on she seemed to gain more interest in everything and much more strength in her legs. She came downstairs again for tea, and afterwards the children played games till supper time.

The next day Dinah spent more or less a normal day. She was still weak, but hour by hour Bessie could see her improving. It seemed like a miracle to William and Mary Jane. They all went to bed tired, but very, very happy.

CHAPTER NINE

GRANDMA OATS – A LITTLE CAMEO

MABEL TREMBATH spent her school holidays with Grandma Oats who lived with her two daughters, Mary Liz and Dinah, in the house on the corner of North Square, Pendeen. Gracie, her sister, was sent up the hill to stay with Grandpa Trembath who lived with his daughter, Great-aunt Trembath, in a square house below the Carn. Her brother Willy and her baby sister Olive, stayed in Penzance, away from home for a change with Aunt Eddy who lived with her two daughters, Grace and Bessy, at the Eastern Green end of the town.

Mabel didn't mind staying with Grandma Oats. She liked the happy-go-lucky times in North Square rather than the upright way Gracie spent at Grandpa Trembath's. Grandma's house was always full of people laughing and joking. They all loved to eat, drink and be merry. Often one or other of the men who came courting would give Mabel a sixpence if they were in favour with one of the girls, to spend as she wished.

Mabel was expected to help with the house-work. She didn't mind it; her free time was her own; she could play with the children who lived in the mine cottages; she could wear what she liked and stay out after dark if she so pleased. She loved to sit outside on the hedge and watch the moon rise above the Carn like a huge round orange.

Poor Gracie had to wear the clothes Great Aunt Trembath chose for her. She always had to put on hat and gloves when going out for a walk, or to Church on Sundays. She was not allowed to play with the village children or go out alone after dark. Her only friend was Gertie Tresize from the big house. The two little girls spent most of their time hiding in an old elder tree at the bottom of the garden watching Mabel and her friends playing on the Carn.

Mabel had to fetch and carry to help Mary Liz, who looked after the house for Grandma Oats and also did all the cooking and cleaning. Dinah, her sister, looked after the linen. She was a frail soul, which was to be expected after her child-hood illness. As well as all the sewing and mending she did the book-keeping.

Mabel could write, spell and add very well for her age, so she helped Dinah in the evenings. Lizzy Tish, the maid of all work, did the washing and scrubbing, and Mrs. Carbines came up from Bowjewyan to help with the ironing.

Dinah and Mabel sat together at the kitchen table, in front of the open doors of the slab, to do the book-keeping. These evenings were the best part of the day for Mabel. The kitchen was very

warm and cosy, the slab brasses shining in the fire light, the kettle singing and the cats, purring, sitting inside the fender. They loved it there and would stare at the flames for hours on end.

When the accounts were done Mary Liz joined them for hot cocoa and baked taties oozing with farmhouse butter before she went up to bed. Aunt Dinah told her stories about the old days. They often talked for so long that they forgot to build up the fire and put the cats out in the rush to get to bed before midnight. There were always ructions the next morning if Mary Liz came down first thing to find a black grate and no hot water, and "cat" all over the place.

While the girls were busy all day Grandma Oats sat in her parlour and did nothing – that is, she did only the things she wanted to do. All her life she had been pampered and spoiled and looked after by someone else – first by her Mother, then Grandpa Oats; after that, Mary Liz and Dinah and now little Mabel. So, through the years she had grown rounder and rounder and more and more rosy – the end of her nose as well as her cheeks. Grandma loved her drop of gin with a lump of sugar in it. Grandpa used to say, before he died, that Grandma ought to be able to see in the dark by the end of her nose. It couldn't have hurt her, for a picture of health she looked. She must have been well over seventy when Grandpa Oats died. Everyone guessed her age, mind you. She never ever breathed a word to anyone how old she really was.

Grandma Oats sat in her parlour in her crimson plush rocking chair, a little soft feather cushion behind her head and a velvet covered one lower down, just right for her back; her feet rested on a round beaded stool made for her by some long dead sailor sweetheart whilst he served his time at sea. Between her and a well built up fire (summer and winter) she had a spindly rosewood table placed just so, by her right hand. It was so cluttered Mabel could never really dust it properly. In the centre stood the family Bible, her prayer book, "Thoughts for today" and a copy of Doctor Roundhead's "Women's Ailments, And How To Cure Them." Nearby were her spectacles, spy glass, a tin of gingerbreads with a portrait of Queen Victoria on the front, a dish of peppermints for her wind, a bottle of gin and her glass hidden under a knitted tea cosy, a daguerreotype of Grandpa Oats in his early twenties and a bottle of smelling salts. She often felt a bit faint, maybe caused by the fire too hot or the gossip too spicy. Grandma Oats loved company. She expected someone every afternoon for tea and someone always came, especially on a wet and windy afternoon.

Grandma Oats was known for her hospitality. She dressed up for the occasion in her next to best navy blue serge dress, her black pinny edged in beaded fringe and her white lace cap with a black velvet bow at the back to show she was a widow – the streamers told how many years she had been widowed by their length. Hers were fairly long, Grandpa Oats had been dead a good many years.

The cameo she wore at her neck was given to her by her Grandmother when she was first engaged – not to Grandpa Oats, he came into her life much later on; it was his brother, Albert, she fell in love with when she was sixteen. They first met at a Hunt Ball in Penzance. Albert was a great horseman, he rode well, but sometimes not too wisely. He tired himself and his horse out at most Meets. One September morning, on a long run after the hounds had met in St. Just Square, he jumped his horse over a small adit. The animal tripped and threw Albert down the shaft. Riders who were following helped him out, but he couldn't stand; his leg was broken. The leg took a long time to mend. Albert had to stay on his back for many months. He was a heavy man and an impatient one. He wanted to run before he could walk; he could not abide staying still for so long. Grandma Oats remembered how her feelings changed during this time towards Albert. Love seemed to have flown out of the window. It wasn't the same somehow. Albert had always been

PENDEEN CHURCH.

such fun to be with. He had altered since the accident. Because he could not get out so much he read a lot. This made him more thoughtful and sober-minded. At sixteen Grandma Oats did not want to stay at home. She was very pretty and loved a good time. The doctor had said Albert's leg would be much shorter than the other, so he would always have a limp.

The poor girl sat with him at home and tried hard to like the things that interested him. She knitted and tatted and chatted about this and that, but knew he wasn't listening; she could tell by his face. One Sunday afternoon she went to see Albert for the last time and told him how she felt.

She gave him back his ring, which he wouldn't take. He didn't seem surprised; in fact she felt he was relieved. He was a great deal older than she was. Maybe he also had had second thoughts.

Grandma looked down at her hands. Her fingers were very fat; his ring wouldn't fit her now. She still had the ring upstairs in her jewel-box; three diamonds and two rubies set in a gold band. Maybe she would give it to Mabel some time for being so helpful.

How long ago it all seemed now. Her family were very upset at the time. They couldn't understand it; it seemed so unkind not to marry a man because he had a limp. They liked Albert and his brother Maddern. Secretly, Grandma also liked Maddern, only she hadn't told anyone. She had got to know him very well when they spent so much time sitting with Albert, and afterwards on many a starlight evening when Maddern walked her the long way home.

In twelve months she and Maddern were married in the new Church of St. John the Baptist under the Carn. Albert went away when his leg got better. He took up with a woman from St. Agnes working as a Bal maiden at Botallack. They sailed for Australia in the New Year. All the village said Grandma was a hard-hearted young woman and ought to be horse-whipped.

Grandma moved uneasily in her chair. She still felt sensitive about what people said. She eased the velvet cushion further down her back which was giving her a lot of trouble in spite of two layers of red flannel around her waist to keep her cheens warm, and six white calico petticoats over that. It still hurt. The doctor said it was rheumatics. He told her she must be very careful of cold draughts and never sleep in a damp bed.

She used to make Dinah put a looking glass between the sheets when they were changed. If it steamed over the bedding was damp so had to be changed again. She would rather sit up all night than sleep in a wet bed.

Her father always carried a potato in his pocket to keep the rheumatics away. Grandma Oats favoured a nutmeg. It became smaller and smaller after being in her pocket for several months, and it did do a bit of good. The best help of all to ease the pain was a good rubbing with horse embrocation once a week. (The blacksmith made it up for her). Up and down and round and round, first to the north and then to the south. Dinah had a lovely soft hand. Mary Liz's hands were rough, but they took it in turns – rub, rub, rub, until grandma glowed all over and smelled like grandpa's old horse.

Sometimes she nodded off after dinner, but always woke up to the sound of voices. She would greet one of her best friends with:

"Come in, my dear. Sit down a bit and tell me all the news. How's your poor old father? Did Mrs. White tell you about Mary Jane and all their goings on? Dinah dear, tell Mabel to bring in the tea and some of that seedy cake Mary Liz baked this morning. And dear, don't forget to draw the curtains before you go. Mrs. Carne, tell me now . . . . ."

Mrs. Carne had a lot to tell; it was well past nightfall before she left for home. Mabel had to take the hurricane lamp to see her to her front door. It was a fair old way to go, right down to beyond the chapel.

After supper Grandma had her toddy of hot gin and sugar. With her stone hot water bottle held firmly to her chest and with the help of the girls, she was carried upstairs to bed. The three of them kissed her good-night, blew out the lamp (she kept a candle alight by her bed in case she wanted to read for a bit), then they softly closed the door and clattered downstairs to the kitchen below.

Tomorrow would be Harvest Festival. Dinah had to finish sewing the dress she was making for Mabel and put a clean collar on her own blouse. They were all going to Church in the morning, not only for the special service and the singing, but to see the fruit, flowers and vegetables and, most of all, the new clothes and hats – especially the hats the congregation would be wearing. Miss Trembath (Mabel's aunt on the other side of the family) was always a triumph on festive occasions. Her hats were superb. Oriental birds sat on nests of roses, cherries good enough to eat dangled from black velvet ribbons. Everybody wondered what she would be decked out in tomorrow. Mabel, Mary Liz and Dinah were all agog to see, so they put out the lamp, put out the cats, locked the back and front doors and went to bed.

GREAT-AUNT TREMBATH'S HAT

GREAT-aunt Trembath had three very nice Christian names, Elizabeth Jane Victoria, but no-one ever called her by them. It was always 'Great-aunt' Trembath – even to her nephews and nieces. She lived with her Father, two cats Puss and Miew (there again they had very nice names, Marigold and Daisy but only answered to the call of Puss and Miew), and a very fat pony called Joe. Joe was always called Joe. Grandpa Trembath would have it no other way. It was alright for his daughter and the cats to be called differently, but Joe was Joe. So there 'twas.

The house that gave them shelter was on the way up to the Carn, looking down on Pendeen village. It was spick and span inside. Great-aunt Trembath saw to that. Grandpa saw to the garden which faced the sea. They both had help. Aggie Stroll, a young girl from Trewellard worked her hands raw for one and sixpence a week indoors. Old Willy Trezise nearly broke his back helping Grandpa outdoors for a quarter of tea and six ounces of shag for five days a week, summer and winter. Great-aunt loved flowers and Grandpa loved vegetables. Both were grown in tidy rows between hedges of Escallonia to keep out the North wind and stray dogs.

Both in their way were lonely. Grandpa missed his wife. Still, he was glad to have his daughter to live with him, but it wasn't the same. His daughter was very pernickety in her ways. Everything had to be just so. Mother hadn't minded if he wore his boots indoors or smoked in the kitchen. Now he had to leave his boots outside, on the doorstep. It was so cold for his feet crossing over the slate floor to the fender for his slippers, and he had to have his pipe and baccy in the stable with Joe.

Still, he had his collection. He loved his butterflies, feathers, birds' eggs and rock specimens. He was now arranging his new show cases in time to show little Gracie when she came to stay. Gracie always came to stay during her school holidays. They both loved having her. His daughter-in-law, Grace, had had a hard time since his son, Maddern died in Africa. He loved her as much as his own daughter and wanted her to stay with them in Pendeen, but she was a proud woman and wanted to make her way in business in Penzance and keep her family with her. He missed her all the same. Little Gracie filled her place. She was coming next week for her summer holidays.

The house was in an uproar – everything topsyturvey and upside down. The windows needed to be sparkling, the granite window sills had to be scrubbed outside and the doorsteps scrubbed and whitewashed. All must be spick and span by the time Gracie arrived at the end of the week. The old man was glad to stay in the garden. The weather was moist and warm – good growing weather. His gladioli would be out just in time for Harvest Festival. Great-aunt Trembath arranged flowers for one of the windows in church; the gladioli would make a fine display. Little Gracie loved the gladioli; she said they were fairy flowers.

Up in the house on the hill Great-aunt Trembath was standing in her bedroom in front of the cheval mirror trying on her new hat. It was the largest she had ever worn, just like an upside-down dinner plate, and all the fashion in Paris her woman's magazine said. It was called a boater. It was very plain but very smart. Tomorrow, at Church she would see what the congregation thought of it.

Little Gracie shared Great-aunt Trembath's bed; the Queen bed she called it. She was asleep now, snuggled down under the pink satin eider-down. She was a lovely child, like a little flower. She would look well in the white serge dress with the black velvet collar and cuffs that Mrs. Tilly, the sewing woman, had made for her. It was hanging over the chair by the bed with her straw sailor hat, white gloves and black buttoned boots. She would be a pretty picture in Church tomorrow.

Great-aunt Trembath sighed and went over to the washing-stand. The water in the jug was still warm; it would do for her to wash in. She emptied the dirty water into the slop bucket and poured out fresh into the bowl. Her thoughts went back to the time when she was young. She wasn't good

looking but had an upright carriage, and her figure was tall and slim. She would have liked to have been married and to have had children, but the chance never came. Before she was twenty her Mother had become ill so she had had to stay at home to take care of her. After her mother died, Great-aunt Trembath couldn't leave her father on his own, so there it was – and still is, she thought. One day she would go abroad, to Canada maybe. Ralph, her nephew, was over there in Montreal. It would be nice to see him and his family again. She cleaned her teeth in sea-salt and water, put on her nightgown, got in beside little Gracie and lay awake thinking until the moon sank below the Carn.

Sunday morning dawned fair and fine. The Trembaths had their breakfast in the dining room beside the window. Gracie loved having breakfast with her Aunt and Grandpa, especially on Sundays. Hot porridge with treacle on it, fried pilchards all crispy and brown from the oven, and fresh baked bread, with home-made butter as yellow as the buttercups on the hedge outside the window. Lots of milky tea to finish, with Red

Rollers, the first of the Cornish apples to ripen before Harvest Festival. She had picked a basketful at the top of the garden with Grandpa, and they had taken some of them with his precious gladioli across to the Church.

Great-aunt was fussing Grandpa and Gracie; she wanted to arrive in Church just at the right moment. Not too early so that there was no-one but the sidesmen to see her entry, and not too late so that the Church was full and her hat would not be seen to the best advantage. The family pew was just behind the vicar's family and Great-aunt Trembath was vain enough to know that all the villagers were agog to see her new hat. What on earth was Gracie doing upstairs? Why was her father going out to the stable at the last moment before they left? Joe was in the field – had he forgotten? They were late. They would have to take the short cut through Miner's Row, an alleyway between overcrowded cottages, and go into Church from the East gate.

At last they were ready. Great-aunt Trembath set off first, clutching her prayer book. Thank goodness there was no wind blowing. In single file they crossed the field, Grandpa following in his Sunday going-to-meeting suit, bowler, and black umbrella just in case it rained. Gracie lagged behind. She felt a bit shy in her new outfit. She would rather go to Church in her everyday clothes and sit at the back – not up in a front pew. She didn't like people looking at her, especially people she knew like Mary Liz and Dinah. She didn't like going through Miner's Row either, it always smelled of dried fish. At this time of year fish was very plentiful; "When corn is in the stocks, fish are in the rocks" was an old saying. So the miners' wives hung their herring, mackerel

MINER'S ROW.

and pilchards on long sticks between forked stakes, on the wall beside their cottage doors, to dry in the sun.

On the way through Miners' Row Great-aunt Trembath found it difficult to keep her new hat on straight; the walls of the cottages were so close together. She wondered how they lived like this – door to door, window facing window, always within earshot of each another. Why hadn't she put on a smaller hat? It was a good job she had put long hat pins in her boater to keep it in place.

"Hurry now, Gracie. I can hear the organ playing. Come on, father!"

Why was he taking so long? Great-aunt Trembath was in a real tizzy. She went through the East gate, down the path and by the time she got to the Church her face was bright crimson, her hat bobbing up and down, and her hair all awry. She opened the door, holding her head high, and swept down the aisle, Grandpa and Gracie following.

Mabel, Mary Liz and Dinah sat in their pew looking towards the door. All the congregation was waiting with them. What would Aunt's hat be like this year? They heard the click of the door latch, there was a slight whiff of fish in the air. Great-aunt Trembath was wearing an enormous plate of a hat; around the brim were three dried pilchards, head to tail, with a fourth hanging jauntily down her back. They couldn't believe their eyes. Birds of paradise, ostrich feathers or Dijon roses . . . but dried fish? What was the world coming to?

Grandpa Trembath was slightly deaf. He sat through the service not hearing the titters that went on around him. Gracie always sat with her eyes shut in Church; she never knew when she should open or shut them so she didn't see the grins on the faces of the choir boys. Great-aunt Trembath was surprised to see the vicar look with astonishment at their pew before he began his sermon. She hadn't expected her hat to cause quite such a sensation.

DOOMED HOUSE UNDER THE GUMP.

CHAPTER ELEVEN

MEMORIES OF THE TREMBATH CHILDREN:
DEATH OF LITTLE JOHNNY

AFTER Maddern Trembath died in Africa his wife, Grace, left Pendeen and made a new life for herself and her family in Penzance. The children took a long time to settle down in the town. They were country children, so missed the happy days of their early childhood.

Little Gracie's memory of that part of their lives was when her baby brother John died. She had heard her aunts say, as they sat in her mother's parlour which was darkened and stuffy by the heavy curtains being drawn before the funeral, that old Mrs. Tiddy had seen all the windows lighted in the empty barren house up under the Gump. This was a sure sign of doom in the family. The house was once the home of their forbears. The last time the lights were seen was when Great Grandpa died at the age of ninety.

Gracie could feel the atmosphere of the room even now; her aunts chatting by the fire, nodding their heads together like three old crows, sitting uncomfortably in their black bombazine bustles and heavy veils, the men of the family uneasy in their best suits, staring at the ceiling. Gracie and her sister, Mabel, had black silk dresses to wear to the funeral, with straw bonnets to match. Willy, their brother, had his first long trousers in black serge. He complained bitterly that they scratched his legs. Gracie knew how he felt. She had the same trouble when sitting on Great Grandma's horse-hair sofa. The sharp wiry little hairs pricked her legs through her calico drawers. Little sister Olive was too young to wear black, so the shoulder straps of her pinafore were tied with black taffeta bows.

The house seemed gloomy and very quiet; Gracie hated the darkened rooms. She was very sad that poor Johnny had died and gone to Heaven; she would be glad when the funeral was over. They had never been to a funeral before. Willy and Mabel and Gracie had talked about it when they were in bed during the night. Willy knew all about funerals; he and his friend, Charley Angwin, had hidden behind the church wall when old Mrs. Teagle had been buried. Men, hats in hand, and women with long black veils over their faces stood around a deep hole in the ground. The parson spoke in a loud voice, but the boys couldn't hear what he was saying because the wind carried away his words whilst the coffin was lowered gently down into the earth. Willy thought they looked sad; one man picked up a handful of earth and threw it into the hole; a woman stepped forward with a sprig of rosemary and dropped it in. Then all turned and followed the vicar, two by two,

OLD PENDEEN CHURCHYARD.

prepared a splendid tea for all the mourners to come back to after the funeral. Some of them stayed very late; some had not gone even yet; Gracie could hear the murmer of voices below, like the hum of drones in a buzza. She lay awake thinking about death. It was a terrible thing being someone and then suddenly no-one, nothing, just blackness forever and evermore. She could hardly cope with the fear in her heart.

Baby John had seemed so small to die. He would never run through a field of hay and feel the softness of green grasses against his legs. He would never lie on his back on the cliff top amongst the sea-pinks and watch the gulls swooping down to the sea. Poor little thing – why had he been born, Gracie wondered; had it been worth all the sorrow and pain? Her heart almost stopped when she thought about it. One day it would happen to her; never, never to be alive again. The parson said in church all good people would one day go to Heaven. Her mother said the streets of Heaven were paved with gold and that, with a great rushing of wings, the angels swooped down and carried you up above the clouds. Grandma Oats said she heard that strange sound above the house the night Johnny had died. Gracie didn't fancy spending the rest of her time pacing up and down golden streets with only angels for company. She wanted always to be with the people, places and things she loved here on earth, but it didn't seem possible. How could the sky hold so many hordes? Gracie felt hot and cold all over in her little white bed; she panicked, lying awake beside her sleeping brother and sisters.

She peeped over her eider-down and saw the moon shining down through the window at her. The moon had such a kind face. Grown-ups called

back to the church. Gracie now knew what was going to happen this afternoon.

At two o'clock the church bell began to toll. It was time to go. Their aunts and uncles gathered up their hats and shawls and walked behind the parson across the fields to the church. Gracie thought how warm the sun felt on her back and how glad she was to be alive and out in the sunlight again.

When Gracie, Mabel, Willy and Olive went to bed that night Gracie stayed awake long after the others had gone to sleep. They were all very tired after an oddly exciting day. Their mother had it the Man in the Moon, but Gracie sometimes wondered if it was the face of God. It certainly calmed her down; she began to feel much better.

Gracie knew one person who gave her the most reasonable answer when she raised the question of death – her Sunday School teacher who was a painter from up country. Gracie loved her paintings and hoped one day to be as good an artist. She told Gracie that dying was just like going to a big strange house, being in a room and going to the door, opening it into another room, going through that door and closing it behind one. Gracie thought things over; she felt better now. The best thing, she decided, was to pray to God for his help and understanding. She believed in God. She could find him everywhere, on the moors, in the trees, the sea, the sky. All the big things spoke of God's presence – and the little things too – a baby's ear, the little pink and yellow shells she found down at Boat Cove, the starry yellow celandines and red tipped field daisies. God would give her an answer. Maybe he would send little Johnny back to earth to tell her what Heaven was really like. This did sometimes happen – Grandma and her aunts were always talking about signs from Heaven and people appearing.

Gracie used to hide under her Father's desk when the grown-ups sat by the fire talking together. No-one knew she was there; as quiet as a mouse she kept. One particular afternoon they were telling a story of such a sign from Heaven happening. A member of the family lived in Penzance – Gracie couldn't catch who – with her two daughters and grandchildren, one of whom was Alice who died when she was very young.

Before she died she used to sleep with her Grandmother in a very large bed with red velvet bobble-fringed curtains tightly drawn around. Grandma liked a bit of company by night as she missed Grandpa when he died. After Alice died, Grandma's other grandchild, Mary Anne, slept in her place. One very warm night Grandma awoke about three o'clock. It was so hot in bed that she drew the heavy curtains back for more air.

Dearey dearey me, someone had left the landing lamp burning – one of the daughters home late, maybe. Grandma pulled the curtains further back to shout to someone. She stopped. There was a small shadowy figure standing in the doorway. It was pale and slim in a white night-gown. It must be Mary Anne sleep-walking again, she'd be over the stairs. The old woman reached down the bed for her paisley shawl, but it wasn't Mary Anne – she was sleeping peacefully by her Grandmother's side. The old woman peered out again towards the door: the landing was in darkness, the figure gone.

THE END HOUSE NORTH SQUARE.

Gracie heard from her cubby-hole her aunts twittering like birds in a tree. They knew the story meant little Alice had come down to earth again to see her Grandma, the one she loved.

Gracie felt sleepy now. She wouldn't be afraid anymore if brother Johnny came back now and then. She didn't mind dying if she could come down from Heaven from time to time and go home to Pendeen, to lie on the warm moorland earth and watch the skylark rising, cloud above cloud, until it also reached Heaven.

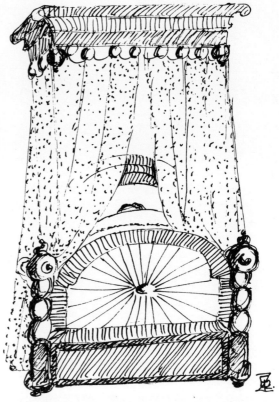

THE QUEEN BED.

ST JUST SQUARE.

A SUNDAY SCHOOL TREAT

MABEL'S memory went back to a hot sunny day in a green field, half way between Pendeen and St. Just, where the annual School Treat was held. What a day it was. The schools of St. Just and Pendeen competed for prizes and for how much everyone could eat. St. Just town band played on and on and the miners' choir from Levant sang their hearts out. The girls in their best white dresses and long black stockings, and the boys in sailor suits, danced the maypole. The small children ran and skipped about. There were games for all; three legged, egg and spoon, sack races, apple bobbing, weight lifting, men throwing yellow sheaves of corn high in the sky competing to see who was the strongest and threw the highest. Ralph Tregear always won; he was the tallest. Major Oats, his cousin, was runner-up; the heaviest man there, he could lift a young cow and hold it above his head.

There were side shows – Aunt Sally's, lucky dips and coconut shies. There were cake stalls, flower stalls, an ice cream cart with cornets with a dob of clotted cream on top. Other stallholders were all around the field selling lemonade, nougat, toffee apples and long pink sticks of rock with Penzance written in a circle inside. How did the writing get there? Mabel loved the ginger pop best of all. It was sold in spiral green glass bottles. She took a long time when she was young to learn how to press her tongue against the ball in the curly neck of the bottle which released a steady flow of fizzy beer down her throat and up her nose. She could feel the twitching, stinging sensation even now. How it made all the children laugh.

Willy had the time of his life with his friends chasing the girls behind the hay stack, catching them there to lift their skirts and see what colour ribbon they had threaded through the legs of their white cotton drawers.

At the end of the day everyone under the age of sixteen had a Sunday School treat saffron bun, which was large, flat and full of currants, given to them. Mabel liked licking the sticky brown sugar which was sprinkled on top. As it was Coronation year they were also given a china mug with a painting of the King's head on one side and his Queen's on the other, surrounded by leaves and flowers. Mabel often wondered, being very young, what happened to the rest of their bodies. Maybe they were so important that they didn't have any, or perhaps they walked about with a covering of fresh flowers every day instead of clothes.

Only whilst the children sat on the grass and

drank milk from the new mugs and ate their buns did the band have a rest for cold pasties, fuggen and cider (served to them by the farmers' wives), on the hay stack in the corner of the field.

Afterwards, when shadows lengthened across the field, the wrestlers held sway; great slippery brown bodies clutching shirts, and swaying till one or the other fell to the grass, a defeated man. Mabel felt sorry for the losers, and clapped and cheered for all of them when the wrestling match was over.

As darkness fell over the coast the flares were lighted, and the field came alive with dancing shadows. The children, tired and happy, climbed up into the waggons, some to sleep and others to watch the grown-ups packing up the tables and forms, plates and mugs, putting them under a tarpaulin to be collected in the morning.

A little shy ring of dancing broke out here and there to the tune of a solitary fiddler. Mabel was reminded of the story she had heard her mother tell so many times, how, one night, a Sunday it was, over Lamorna way some boys and girls had danced in a ring to the tune of a merry fiddler. It was a dreadful thing to do – frowned on by Church and Chapel alike – to dance on a Sunday. Poor things, they were carried away by the full moon and the fairy music. By midnight they were all turned to stone. They still stand there to this day. The fiddler hopped over the hedge and away, but he didn't get far; he was caught and turned to stone in the next field. Mabel hoped this would not happen to her friends and relations; it was almost midnight, and tomorrow was Sunday. Just in time the flares were doused.

The grown-ups climbed into the waggons after the children. Under the light of the moon they sang their way home behind the plodding horses – some east to Pendeen, and some west to St. Just.

CHAPTER THIRTEEN

GRANDPA TREMBATH:
A CHILD WITHIN A MAN

LITTLE Olive's memory was short, but she remembered best of all Grandpa Trembath. A small square man he was, with twinkling blue eyes and greying beard that tickled her nose when she kissed him. He would take her onto his knee and spend endless time explaining about his collections.

Olive loved birds, and Grandpa had some beautiful ones in domed glass cases around his study – this room was full of interesting things. He had special cabinets made by the local carpenter, with glass lined drawers one on top of the other, each one containing an eyeful of beauty. Birds eggs and feathers – not only from Cornwall, but from almost all over the world that his friends had brought back from Australia, Africa and America. One egg was as big as a pudding basin. It was an ostrich egg, he told her, from a long legged bird with a long, long neck and black beady eyes. It could run faster than any man.

Grandpa also collected butterflies and moths, some with wings as blue as the sky and some as grey as Old Man's Beard. On the mantelpiece was a picture of a little Dutch boy and girl made up from beautifully coloured butterfly wings. Grandpa said it would be hers one day. Minerals too, he had, diamonds, crystals and fool's gold. He used to allow Olive to open the drawers and choose one thing at a time, then he would tell her a story about it.

On this day she chose a blue-black bully from Portheras beach which Grandpa used as a doorstop to keep the study door ajar so that he could hear what Great-aunt Trembath and Aggie Twitch were on about in the kitchen.

Grandpa looked at the sea-polished stone for a long time, then sat down in his favourite chair and lifted Olive onto his knee. She knew exactly what was going to happen – he was going to take off his spectacles, breathe hard on each side of them and then take a large white handkerchief from his breast-pocket and polish the glasses until they shone. Just why he did this she never understood because he was going to tell her a story, not read her one. However, she never questioned why he did it, so after he had blown his nose very hard and seen that she was comfortably settled, he would then begin:-

"Lying low under the cliff, above Portheras beach, two cottages stood together between grey granite rocks, part of which made up their walls. A stream fell away to the sea from their very door step and the land was so steep to east and west that they felt no wind, only the spray which came

spluttering up the zawn on hard winter nights. No trees grew there, only low blackthorn and gorse bushes between the rocks.

"In the cottages lived two brothers, Gerval and Moss. Gerval, the elder, begat a son – Elvin – while Moss had a daughter – Tarn. Both children were born strong and beautiful and grew up as brother and sister. They spent their days in the sea and on the beach helping with the boats. Mending the nets was Tarn's job; endless hours she sat by the boat-house door in the sun, closing home the holes with a shoemaker's needle and binder twine.

Elvin patched the lobster pots with withies which were planted by the edge of the stream for this very purpose.

"As the children grew, so love blossomed within their hearts for each other, and before seventeen summers had passed they had become man and maid.

" "Forever." they whispered as they lay amongst the long grasses on the cliff top.

"Their parents watched knowingly and were pleased. Life would go on in the cottages for a lot longer yet.

"Gerval and Moss took Elvin with them in their charlock-yellow boat when they went to sea with the rest of the men who fished from Boat Cove. Tarn was not allowed to go. Neither she nor her mother nor her aunt were permitted to set foot in a working boat. It was ill luck for a crew to take a woman, a cat or a parson when they went to sea. For this reason the brothers kept a dinghy so that they could all go out for jaunts on summer Sunday afternoons when the sea was calm and the swallows flying high – a sign, they said, of prolonged fine weather. Fishing, too, was good at such times. The men lived by their master (the sea), and the weather. In winter, when the choughs flew in circles overhead and the gulls skimmed and screeched across the bay, the men would sleep soundly at night, for they would not set sail till the oncoming storm had ceased.

"Tarn loved the choughs with their great black wings and red beaks and feet. They were always fussing and scolding each other under the cliff where her favourite rock stood among the gorse and bracken. She would sit for hours below the rock on summer evenings and winter afternoons watching and waiting for the first boat to appear. If it was charlock-yellow she was off down the path and along the shore to help Elvin, her father and Uncle Moss to unload the catch.

"Sometimes she was sent up to the fields early in the morning to be on the look-out for shoals of herring. She would see them flashing in the sunlight as though a great silver cloud had fallen from the sky onto the surface of the sea. At such times Tarn's cry, "Heava!" clear as a bell, floated down to the waiting men on the beach below. At seventeen she was as brown as a berry and tall and slim as a withy. Her hair, black as the night, fell to her waist in a great swinging coil which she braided with a yellow ribbon that Elvin had brought back for her from the Corpus Christi fair which came to Penzance every June. Her eyes were of no colour in particular. Her parents claimed that they were grey, but Elvin knew that they could be wild violet-blue on a summer's evening when they reflected the sky above, or the deep, deep purple of a rock pool when her mad was up and she flared at him across the winter's fire.

"Elvin was stocky, his skin almost black from being always exposed to the sun and wind. His hair was mahogany-red and fell to his shoulders in seemingly always wet ringlets. The brine from the sea kept it that way his parents said. His eyes were blue; all sailors have blue eyes from looking at the sea and sky all day long. His back was strong and he could lift a full barrel of brandy and carry it up the cliff path, never pausing to put it down for a rest. Not many Boat Cove men could do that. His father and mother were proud of him, for he was a good lad and they hoped that he would stay in the cove and marry Tarn and that soon, very soon, there would be the sound of grandchildren's voices echoing down the zawns and through the caves, vying with the wind.

"Tarn's parents also hoped for such a match, although secretly her mother daydreamed of a wealthy squire coming down to the cove and whisking Tarn away on a splendid white stallion. If this happened too many hearts would be broken and Tarn might be lost to them forever, so she put the dream wish firmly away to the back of her mind."

Grandpa Trembath eased Olive over from one knee to the other; she was a heavy little thing for her age and his knees weren't as young as they used to be – in fact . . . Grandpa pulled himself up sharply. This would never do. If he started thinking about himself and his rheumatics he would forget where he had got to in the story, so:

"One late September afternoon Tarn was sitting beside her rock watching for the menfolk to come back when she saw something thrashing about in a gorse bush lower down the cliff. As the

THE BOAT HOUSE.

"Tarn made soft cooing sounds and gently stroked its feathers. The bird had been caught in a gin – a loop of wire, a length of rope and a wooden peg made up this horrible contraption. Tinkers and gypsies used this method of catching many a supper; farmers used a gun. Tarn loathed all the ways of killing – crude traps most of all. She had in her time released many poor field and wood creatures from snares. It was easy to free this one. It was so exhausted that it didn't even struggle. Tarn felt that in some strange way it knew she was trying to help.

"Loosening the loop she took the trapped leg out carefully and was relieved to find that nothing was broken. On turning the bird over it lay for a few minutes in the grass, then, flapping its wings, it was up and away into the blue above.

"Tarn saw the boats were nearly in so she made haste down the cliff path, following the chough which had joined its fellows swirling, chattering and flashing above her head.

WHEL COVE.

boats were nowhere in sight she clambered down through the heather towards the bush, hearing faint cries of distress as she got nearer.

" "It must be a rabbit," she thought "caught in a snare." But as she parted the bush she found two beady eyes full of fear and resentment looking up at her. It was a Cornish chough, lying on its back exhausted, its flaming claws fluttering in the air.

"For the rest of the summer the great black bird would come to meet her whenever she went up to her rock to wait for the boats or dream the afternoon away. At first it was for a second or two only, resting on a rock or darting between the sea-pink cushions on the cliff edge. Tarn encouraged it by coaxing and throwing little pieces of bread and bacon that she had saved from her dinner. She talked to it, told the bird about her love for Elvin and about her great fear that one day she would lose him to that cruel and demanding master, the sea. The chough would sit and listen with its head on one side, occasionally flapping its blue-black wings and hopping from one rock to another.

"The days shortened and grew grey and misty. Winter came suddenly, scudding up the zawns, sending sparks down the chimley and burning holes in the rag rug in front of the open fire. Tarn now had an extra job of work to do. She had to collect furze from the moors and driftwood from the beach so that the cottage could be kept warm and bright during the long winter evenings. There was scant time for her to go up to her rock, but her faithful chough found her wherever she happened to be."

Little Olive knew this love story almost by heart. Getting down from her grandfather's knee, she went to the window in the hope that she would see choughs flying around the house, but the mist was low over Pendeen and the sky invisible.

"Tell me more," she demanded and once again perched herself on the old man's knee. It was getting on for tea-time, so Grandpa decided to shorten the story.

"One black Thursday in November a huge storm blew up. Day became as dark as night and

people could hardly make themselves heard above the howling wind and roaring sea. The day before had been a calm one and Elvin, his father and Uncle Moss, together with the other Cove boats had gone to sea as usual. When night fell, and they had not returned, the womenfolk got together; they were alarmed. Some could see lowering clouds on the horizon and the sea becoming inky blue. White horses were already riding the waves as they raced towards the shore. There was nothing anyone could do but wait.

"At first Tarn's mother built up the fire and hung fresh dry clothes above it. Her aunt made swede and leekie broth in a much used iron saucepan, and put it on one side of the slab in readiness. Tarn kept watch at the window. She could not open the front door, the wind was so strong against it. They all sat by the fire and turned to their knitting.

"Three days went by. Many times Tarn struggled up the cliff path, seeking some sight or sound of something hopeful, but the wind blew her backwards and the spray stung her eyes so that she could hardly find her way back home to the cottages.

"Inside, the womenfolk knew there was little hope – no boats could stand such a battering. All now sat listless together, hands in their laps, nursing their own fears.

"Monday's dawn brought forth a watery sun, with the sky clearing away to the west over St. Just. Tarn got up, dressed and made her way out of the back door, trudging tearfully up the path to her rock. Today she would know if Elvin had been drowned.

"The choughs for once were silent, hidden in their cliff-side holes. One or two gulls swooped and screamed over her head. She stood by her rock, straining her eyes, trying to peer through the cloud of spume and spray. There was no sign of anything either on land or water, just an awful silence between the breaking of waves on the shore. Then, suddenly, she heard the flapping of wings and a hoarse cry. There was her chough, swooping down from above to land at her feet.

"At first Tarn thought the bird was distressed by the gale, but it seemed to be trying to attract her attention to come down the path to the beach. It hopped a few paces, turned around, squawked, waited, then flew a little way and perched on a stone.

"Tarn knew it all signified something, so she followed quickly. As she turned the corner of the cliff she could see that the tide was going out, the beach littered with seaweed and debris. The chough flew down to the water's edge and hopped onto a large granite boulder. Floating nearby Tarn could see a charlock-yellow plank with something strapped onto it. She ran on in horror, stumbling over the wet pebbles along the beach, sure it was Elvin. Was he alive? She dared not think.

"A huge green wave rose and crashed onto the shingle. The charlock-yellow plank rose with

it and landed almost at her feet. It WAS Elvin. Face downward he lay, bound and bedraggled. Tarn tore at the waterproof covering; the chough pecked and pulled at the orange binder twine. Waves crashed and swamped them both, flinging sand bullies at them, blinding her and stinging her body . . .''

"Father! Father! Come quick!" Great-aunt Trembath tore into the room. "Joe's loose and got out of his field. He's up in Mrs. Pascoe's meadow, trampling all over her broccoli. Olive, run and fetch Arthur next door to help catch him – you can go quicker than your Grandpa."

Grandpa Trembath went puffing towards the door, little Olive just in front of him. She wanted to hear the end of the story once again although she knew it off by heart. It had a secret, just like the seventh magpie: "Seven for a secret that's never been told."

Olive loved all birds as much as her Grandpa. They spent many happy hours together walking on the cliffs watching them, and picking the wild flowers. One of Grandpa's brothers described him as "a child within a man." She loved her grandfather very much. She missed him terribly when her family moved to Penzance. He gave her a little mother-of-pearl purse on a chain when she left. He had brought it back from Paris many years before. Olive thought if only she were a bird, she could spread her wings and fly to Paris, or anywhere else in the world where her Grandpa and his friends had been. Best of all, she could fly back to Grandpa at Pendeen and live with him forever.

60

CHAPTER FOURTEEN

CRIB AND CROWST

WILLY'S memories were different again. Mabel and Gracie always took crib and crowst down to the mine for their Father on Saturdays. Sometimes he and Olive were allowed to go with them.

The day before this particular Saturday morning the first traction engine came through the village on its way to Levant mine. All the villagers lined the roadside to greet it, waving flags and cheering. It was a grand sight. Willy and his sisters sat in Grandma Oats' front window; they had a wonderful view, it was very exciting. First came a man from St. Just, a Mr. Bright. Willy knew his name because he had heard his father and their neighbours talking about him the night before: a proper lady's man he was. Willy didn't know what this meant, but he felt it was something important in the grown-ups world. Mr. Bright walked about ten paces in front of the puffing and steaming engine, waving a red flag to keep the children from running under its wheels. It rattled along the road at a fair ole pace, black iron and yellow brass gleaming in the sunshine. A polished bell, hanging from the roof of the cab, was pulled by the driver as he turned the corner. There was a clashing of metal, clamour from the bell, two hoots of the steam-whistle and then, with a great roar from the crowd, the engine was gone, rolling and rumbling down the hill to the mine. No-one had ever seen such a mighty and beautiful monster in Pendeen before. It made everyone's day and was talked about by the the villagers for many months afterwards.

Grandpa Trembath was manager of Levant mine. On Saturday morning, the children took crib and crowst down to the Count House to him. Willy was all agog to go and see the traction engine working at the face of the mine.

At nine o'clock, after breakfast, off they set with pasties and heavy cake in a wicker mawn, covered with a white cloth. For drink, they took cold tea in a milk can. Their Mother gave them the usual warnings:

"Don't drop the mawn, or swing the milk can of cold tea over your shoulder round and round like a windmill."

Willy hung his head. He had done this many times to see if the tea spilled out, but he hadn't known his Mother was watching him.

"Don't fall down the open adits on the way. Don't go near the mine workings. Don't pick any blackberries because it's after the 29th September, and the Devil will have pee'd on them."

Mable and Gracie carried the mawn between

them. Little Olive took her skipping rope with the bells, and skipped behind them. Willy was well ahead, running on and running back to them just like their dog, Bessy, did when she sometimes came on their walks. She wasn't allowed to come this morning because she would chase the cows and bark at the waggon horses.

Willy saw many juicy blackberries out of the corner of his eye, but couldn't stop to pick them. Maybe on his way home, in spite of what his Mother said, he would find a good straggle of ripe ones and could shout over the edge of the brambles at his sisters – or anyone else who passed

by – not to come near him and steal his place:

"Cuddy Cuddy – I O!
Who comes near me
Will have a black eye-o!"

When they got to the top of the hill, and looked down, they could see the mine workings spread before them like an open red gash in the landscape. The granite rock and chocolate brown earth seemed to be covered with a fine pink and blue cloud.

"Just like Great-aunt Tregear's opal engagement ring." Willy thought as he looked at it.

The sea was sienna red below the cliffs, stained by the tin ore, the cliffs streaming with viridian green copper runnels and the sun dancing on the sea like a million diamonds. Men, horses and machines working everywhere were a sight to see.

"Just like bees." Willy thought; and there, in the middle, was the traction engine, like the Queen Bee.

He could see his father as they got nearer, standing in the doorway of the Count House talking to a dozen or more men in a circle around him. Other men were in groups with their heads together. Suddenly Willy realised that the mine was strangely quiet. The big beam was silent; all the to-ing and fro-ing they had seen from the top had suddenly ceased.

As soon as the children's father saw them coming down the hill he left the group of men and came to meet them. Straight away he sent them into the Count House. Willy noticed that the blinds were pulled down, which was odd at this time of day.

"I'm going to have my crowst in here" his father said "just for a change."

The girls didn't seem to mind – they could play with the cats on the window sill – but Willy was very disappointed. He liked sitting outside in the sun watching the miners working. Sometimes the men would come over to chat, and if he was lucky, give him a piece of fuggen or a corner of pasty which he hoped would be the sweet end, for in those days pasties were divided into sweet (apple, treacle. mincemeat, jam) and savoury (meat, taties, turnip, onion) halves.

While their father was having his crowst men came in and out, whispering to him over the table. Willy could not hear all of what they were saying; he gathered there had been a nasty accident; a man had been killed. It was old deaf Mike who hung about the mine doing odd jobs. Poor old chap. He didn't hear the traction engine behind him, and it had crushed him into the road just like a fly, one man said. That's why all the blinds were drawn and why his Father was eating his crowst in the Count House; it was done so that his sisters wouldn't see the awful sight.

Willy wanted to ask his father all sorts of questions; he knew he mustn't. His father looked

tired. Willy knew the traction engine had cost a lot of money and meant great improvements in the mine. He also knew the miners to a man would be against using it after this tragic accident. So Willy said to his sisters:

"Come on, let's go home early and pick some blackberries. We can fill the mawn if we go back by the lane, and Mother can make a tart for our tea."

They ran out of the back door and along the cliff path. Willy thought he would burst if he didn't tell them about poor old deaf Mike. He did tell, and when they heard about it Gracie and Mabel wanted to go back to see what had happened. Willy said no at first, because he thought of his father and what trouble he had taken to shield them, but with a little persuasion from the girls he gave way. He was surprised how blood-thirsty they were. Mabel said perhaps there would be blood all over the grass and Gracie thought there would be some hairs sticking to the great wheel. Even little Olive seemed quite keen, so they turned back down the path.

The sun had gone behind a cloud and grey-black mists were rolling in from the sea. The sienna pink now took on a gory colour. Willy suddenly felt cold and a bit sick.

"I don't think I want to go back." he said.

"Cowardy, cowardy, custard." the girls sang, but Willy ran away up the cliff path and back home.

He didn't want to go down to the mine with his father's crib and crowst for a very long time after that.

CHAPTER FIFTEEN

A NEW WORLD

GRACE TREMBATH left Pendeen for Penzance in the early summer with her four children, a tin trunk, a few sticks of furniture, a little navy-blue bag of gold sovereigns and the well-wishes of her friends and relations. It was a complete new world they entered; a world of hurrying, scurrying people, dusty roads, noise and confusion – or so it seemed to the family from the peaceful fields and clifftops of their mining village.

Grace set her bags down inside the door of her new home after the carrier had dropped her. She could hear his horse's hooves clattering by as he took the children on to their Aunt Bessie's at the Eastern Green end of town. They were staying with her relatives for a week to give Grace time to move in.

As the dust settled back on the window panes and the sound of the carrier's horses died away down the street, Grace sat on the tin trunk in utter despair. After the bustle of packing and the excitement of the journey it now seemed she must face the future alone, and make the best of it. It was no good sitting there in the empty room blubbing away like a schoolgirl. She must pull herself together, stop crying and get on with it. Clean the windows for a start. Her tears had made her bodice front all wet. She must look a sight for sore eyes, she thought, as she found her hankie and blew her nose.

She must make some order somewhere, and where better to start than the room she was in. She looked around at it. The room was long and narrow with two windows facing the street, a fireplace with an iron grate at one end and a slab at the other.

"It must have been two rooms at one time." Grace thought. She could see by the floor that one half was quarry slate and the other red laid brick. In fact, it could have been two houses.

A door by the slab opened into a bully-cobbled passage which led to the front door. To the left a door led into a smaller room which had a shop window in it and, to the right, was a door leading into the kitchen which contained another large slab, a copper and an indoor pump for water.

Grace had been into Penzance several times to look at the property. She knew the plan almost by heart. The back stairs led up from the kitchen to three bedrooms of good size. The front stairs were by the main door, contained in a sort of cupboard which led up to two bedrooms and a small room which could be made into a wash-room. It was well planned for what Grace had in

mind. It was nice of Charlie Rowe to let her have it for such a low rent. He seemed a good young man. A pity his wife, Ellen, was an invalid; he was so upright and strong looking with his black hair and blue eyes. Quite dashing, Grace thought. The Eddy family told Grandpa Trembath that the eating house was to let. She was lucky to get it. She knew her father-in-law had saddled his horse and ridden into Penzance the very next day to pay the first month's rent so that he could be sure that she was alright for a bit. This was all unknown to Great-aunt Trembath. The family rift was still as strong as ever. He made the excuse that he was going to market to change the pony for a young horse, a cob maybe, seeing Joe the pony was getting on a bit and he, Grandpa, was getting stouter every day.

Not that he would ever change Joe, thought Grace. That animal was the apple of his eye.

When Maddern, her husband, died out in Africa Grace knew she must start a business

somewhere to make money to keep body and soul together. Her idea was to run an eating-house and take in a lodger or maybe a few paying guests from time to time. The house and shop in Alverton seemed the very place to start.

She was startled out of her daydreams by a tap on the window. She could see a worried face peeping in through the grime. Grace straightened herself, went to the front door and opened it. A poor little soul, like a picked bird, stood on the step; wispy grey hair shoved under an old tam-o-shanter, a small brown face. Two huge black eyes smiled at Grace. An enormous grey knitted garment shrouded her body from neck to hem where two over-size army boots stuck out, seemingly at very odd angles.

"You must be Mrs. Trembath." the woman said. "I'm Mrs. Poldavy, your nearest neighbour across the court at the back. Is there anything I can do for 'ee? You must be clammed. Come round to your back door, I'll make a cup of tea and pass it in."

Grace smiled. "Thank you, m'dear." she said as she shut the door. She went down the passage and unlocked the back door which opened into the court, as Mrs. Poldavy called it.

Grace could see that two rows of cottages faced the back of her property. There was another water pump in the middle of the square, and in one corner an odd little house with the door partly open. The water closet, Grace guessed. How many shared it? she wondered. The whole place reeked of carbolic, stale fried food and cats.

Mrs. Poldavy came out of the end cottage with a cup of tea. Another woman followed with a plate of buns.

"This is Mrs. Carthewy." Mrs. Poldavy said. Another woman appeared with a bowl of sugar and a spoon. ". . . and this is Mrs. Trewinnard. We've all lived here in the Court, as we call it, for a good many years, and our mas and das before us. We've got twenty-seven children between us, and only one man left. Nellie's husband is still alive – if you can call it that. He's boozed up most of the week. The rest of the time he's asleep."

The twenty-seven children were coming out from what seemed to Grace like the very holes in the walls. A pretty girl came forward and gave Grace a bunch of withered dandelions. A boy, older than the rest, asked Grace if she had any children. She said four, and told him their ages. They all seemed so pleased to welcome her amongst them that she felt much better. She'd be alright now, among these Court people.

As she turned back into her new home she thanked them and thought, as she closed the door, of what her husband, Maddern, used to say about the miners up at Pendeen: "They are poor and have nothing to give but their kindness." Maddern! She still missed him so much, but here in Penzance there were no memories, and maybe her loss would ease in time.

Grace went back to the centre room. This would be the dining room, with the serving table and sideboard at one end. The smaller room would be the office and receiving room.

She unpacked some of the bags, but the trunk was too heavy to lift. Whyever hadn't she asked the carrier to take it upstairs when he'd taken up the beds and the bedroom suite that had belonged to her mother? She'd go up now and make the bed.

She got half way up the stairs when there was a knock at the front door. This time it was Charlie's errand boy carrying a box of groceries with all she would need to start. How kind Charlie was. She gave the boy a penny and sent him back with her message of thanks. Under the cover was a bunch of Parma violets and a note. The smell of the flowers took Grace back to the year she was married; Maddern had given her a bunch when he came back from town. Violets didn't grow up Pendeen way, Gulval and Lamorna Valley were the places they did best in.

By five o'clock things were a bit straight. Her next visitors were her two cousins from the Eastern Green end of town. Bessie was very inquisitive, poking her nose in all the corners, while Gracey was full of fun and helpful suggestions. Grace made a cup of tea and cut some ham sandwiches. She was surprised how clammed she was.

Bessie took a sandwich and went upstairs to look at the view from the back. St. Michael's Mount could just be seen over the chimney pots. Gracey asked the cousins if they had a washing

stand for the children's room – they couldn't come down to the back kitchen to wash in the early morning. If Bessie hadn't got one, Aunt Eddy had – in the back house at home. Cousin Gracey suggested that she and Grace carried it up after dark. No-one would see them in the back lane, and her mother would never know.

After the cousins left Grace locked and barred the doors, and went upstairs to bed. She didn't need a candle as the gas street lamp shone right into her bedroom window. She was tired, but not too unhappy.

The following weeks were busy ones. The children settled in. They missed the country, but there were so many things to see that were new. As soon as it was light the water-waggon came along the road, spraying from side to side to keep the dust down during the day. At dusk the lamplighter went his rounds, lighting the gas lamps outside their window with a long pole which had a flame on the end. There were the horse-drawn cabs on the rank at the end of the road; these looked very smart with their black paint and brass fittings. There were new shops to explore, the butter market off Chapel Street, the cattle market at the top of Causewayhead, the bandstand on the Promenade where the brass and silver bands played every weekend. Such fun to sit and listen.

Thursday was market day; the town was full of farmers and their wives. Grace was busy and made much more money on this day. Most of her friends dropped in for a chat, and brought friends and relations who stayed for a meal. She soon had a reputation for good food, drink and comfort.

Grace did well in her first year. She paid all her debts and opened an account at the new Lloyds Bank. Mabel and Gracie went to school in Chapel Street, Willy and Olive to the Infants' at St. Mary's. Mrs. Poldavy and Mrs. Carthewy helped Grace with the cooking and cleaning. Mrs. Trewinnard's eldest girl, Emily, helped wait at table. Mabel, always good at figures, made out the bills. Gracie cleaned the silver and talked prettily to the farmers who often gave her a coin and patted her curly head. This made Mabel so mad. Why should Gracie be made such a fuss of, just because she had black curly hair? Mabel's hair was as straight as a candle; if she wanted curls Emily did it up in rags, and she had to endure a sleepless night as they were so knobbly and uncomfortable.

One day Grace went visiting, and Emily took Olive and Willy to the park. Mabel suggested that she and Gracie should play barbers. They had seen men having their hair cut and moustaches trimmed at Mr. Trezise's shop down the road. Little Gracie sat in the highchair like a lamb whilst Mabel tied a white towel round her neck, took her mother's scissors and comb from the dressing table and

approached Gracie with a very determined look on her face. Little did Gracie know what was in her sister's mind till she saw her raven locks floating down to the floor. Luckily Emily came back early and caught Mabel in time to save one side of Gracie's hair.

"You're looking like a pig with one ear. Mercy me, what is the Missus going to say? You're a bad girl to ruin your sister's looks."

When Grace came back she decided to do the best possible thing, so she cut off the other side. Poor Gracie had to wear a little blue bonnet Emily knitted for her until her hair grew a bit.

Mabel suffered too that week. She had a pair of black buttoned boots which were her pride and joy. They were polished daily and kept under her bed at night. One morning Mabel woke up to find her boots were gone. She couldn't believe her eyes. She had placed them by the gosunder the night before with new laces in, all ready for Sunday School. She put her slippers on and rushed downstairs to ask the grownups if they had seen them. Her Mother was sitting having her breakfast in the kitchen when Mabel asked. She calmly replied yes, she had given them to Gertie, Mrs. Poldavy's daughter, who was the same age and size as Mabel.

Mabel was so angry she was beside herself. She screamed and screamed and thumped on the table till the dishes rattled and fell all over the place.

"My beautiful black buttoned boots. Why? Why? Why?"

Her mother replied that Gertie had no boots or shoes to wear to Chapel, and she was singing in the choir. Mabel had several shoes and boots, so she must give up one pair.

"But not my best black boots!" cried Mabel.

It was no good. All the ranting and raving made no difference. The boots were given away and that was that. Grace continued to eat her breakfast. Mabel sat down and started to cry. Emily took the salt box and put a handful of salt on the fire to keep the angry thoughts away. As the fire burned green Mabel found her anger dying. She stopped crying and went upstairs to change for Sunday School.

Grace Trembath got to know her regular customers well. Some of them were great characters. They came to her for food and comfort; she in return received help and advice.

The most educated man, who came once a week for a plate of cold silver-side and a glass of claret, was very tall with a long brown face and the blue eyes of a sailor. He swept into the dining room in a flowing black cape on Fridays. He always sat at a small table by the fire. He would silently eat his beef and pickles and maybe apple tart and cream, then call Grace over for a chat and a glass of port with his bread and cheese. He knew every tree and stone in West Penwith, every cave and hill. He would tell her many legends she had never heard before. He always left before closing-time, ending with the same words; "One day, in years to come, the voices and music I hear when I am walking on Rosewall Hill will be captured in a little black box, and everyone will hear these sounds in their own back parlours. You won't hear them maybe, Mrs. Trembath, but your children will."

With a click of his heels and a bow from the waist he would sweep to the door and out into the night. Grace never knew where he went or where he slept, but she could see him in her mind, lying amongst the heather, looking up at the stars on top of some moor between Sancreed and Morvah.

Another man, bandy as a coot, Mr. Arthur Trevosson, ate most Saturday lunchtimes with Grace. He was a man with a trouble. His wife had been in her bed for four years. Four years ago she had said she was 'feeling proper poorly and she best go up to lie down for a bit.' She had never come downstairs again. A kind neighbour and her daughter looked after her in the daytime, and he did what he could by night. They lived at Cripplesease; he worked in the quarry at Castle-an-Dinas, so had a long and tiring day and, sometimes, a troublesome night. He never complained. He only wanted to talk to someone like Grace. He just couldn't understand what had happened to his happy, busy, bustling wife. One weekend Grace missed his coming in. Two or three weeks went by. Then, one Saturday lunch-time, in he came full of smiles. He had such good news to tell. He had been away to Falmouth to

cousins for a week's holiday with his wife who was on her feet again, just like she used to be. He almost couldn't believe it. One evening about three weeks before, he was coming down the hill towards his cottage when he noticed smoke coming out of the chimney. As he drew nearer a good smell was floating out of the door. The cat was sitting on the doorstep with a fresh saucer of milk and his dog was chewing a bone on the mat. They were both content and not mewing and yapping as usual when he came home. The door was open and there, to his joy, was his wife in a clean pinny, cooking his supper. She turned and welcomed him with a smile, and chatted during the meal as if nothing had ever happened. The next day she was up with the dawn birds and worked all day long with a will. She never mentioned her long stay in bed, and he didn't either. Their life was back as usual, except for the memory of that wonderful week in Falmouth.

Some of Grace's clients were not kind men. One was a " proper old pest" Emily would say. He always made a mess at table, complained about the food – the beef overdone or underdone, or the beer too weak – spat on the floor mising the spitoons on purpose, and tried to put his hand up Emily's skirt. Worst of all, he got very drunk, weak beer or no, and shouted his complaints at the top of his voice so that people sitting at other tables could hear. One Thursday Mrs. Trewinnard from next door announced:

"I'll bake 'e a pasty he'll never forget."

She got up early the next day and made a good dollop of pastry, told Emily to fetch the po from under the bed upstairs, cut up plenty of potato, turnip and onion, added the contents of what Emily brought her, rolled out the pastry, filled the pasty, salt and peppered it and popped it into the oven.

The old man arrived late, demanding hot roast beef, potato, broccoli and carrots. Grace said she was sorry, but the hot meal was sold out. She only had cold ham and pickles at this time of day. He swore at Grace, sat down at the table and said he wouldn't budge an inch till she served him what he ordered. Grace stood her ground till Mrs. Trewinnard came in with her pasty on a plate. She passed the old man sitting at his table, as if to serve someone further down the room. As she went by, he pulled her back by her pinny strap.

"That's for me," he said and snatched the pasty off the plate and started to wolf it down.

The first mouthful was enough. He turned bright red, then purple and then a sickly green. He staggered up and made for the door, spitting out pasty all over the place. Grace and Mrs. Trewinnard winked at each other and started to clear up the mess.

"We shan't see that old varmint again" said Emily. She took the brush from Grace's hand, sprinkled a handful of salt on the floor and swept it out of the door after him. "He's gone for good this time."

When the dishes were washed the women sat around the table with their last cup of tea and had a good laugh till the tears streamed down their faces.

Dinah, Grace's sister, came to join them with a net of blackbirds for next day's pie, so they told her all about it. Thanks to Mrs. Trewinnard and Emily Grace had managed to do something she had been trying to do for many a month – forget the past and enjoy the future.